Rejoicing in Our Midst

Religious Festivals Round The World

D. G. Butler

Headmaster, West Denton High School, Newcastle upon Tyne

Edward Arnold

© D. G. Butler 1980

First published 1980
by Edward Arnold (Publishers) Ltd
41 Bedford Square, London WC1B 3DQ

British Library Cataloguing in Publication Data

Butler, D G
   Rejoicing in our midst.
   1. Religious calendars
   I. Title
   291.3'6   BL590

   ISBN 0-7131-0478-3

Text set in 11/13 VIP Palatino by Preface Ltd., Salisbury, Wilts.
and printed in Great Britain by
Spottiswoode Ballantyne Ltd., Colchester and London

Preface

Most of the pieces in this book began life as late-night talks on television. I am grateful to Maxwell Deas, Director of Religious Programmes at Tyne Tees Television for allowing me to adapt them for use in a wider context.

I hope that they will be useful to headteachers, at assembly, and also in the classroom. They are arranged by months, with grouping by religions given at the end of the text. It is impossible to date all but a very few with any precision, and it follows that any order of festivals is bound to be quite arbitrary.

For those who wish to treat the theme of the readings more fully, I have added suggestions for a visual symbol for each talk and also some suitable music. Further advice and information is readily available from either of the following organisations:

The SHAP Working Party, 7 Alderbrooke Road, Solihull, West Midlands B91 1NH
The Commission For Racial Equality, Elliott House, 10–12 Allington Street, London SW1E 5EH

I must make special mention of Desmond Brennan, who annually compiles the Calendar of Festivals for the Commission: to him I am especially indebted.

From the inception of the television project to the submission of the scripts, I have been most spendidly helped by Joyce Ferguson, Evelyn McKenzie and Audrey Hill: I should like to express my thanks to them and to my many advisers and friends in the Tyne and Wear Community Relations Council.

Donald Butler
1980

Contents

The dates of most festivals vary considerably from year to year. This grouping into months is only for convenience, and the *order* of festivals is quite arbitrary.

1

Birthday of Guru Gobind Singh (Sikh)

'Sikhs remember their tenth great Guru' (January)

Symbol: Ekonkar

Music: 'Duhn', Side 2, Track 1 from 'This is the Music of India', Philips 6460 854.

Next to their founder, Guru Nanak, the man who is the subject of this talk is the most revered Guru in the minds of a great many Sikhs who celebrate his birthday. Within the space of only forty-two years (1666–1708), Guru Gobind Singh made Sikhism what it is today. It is sadly typical of world history that he died at the hands of an assassin.

One of his memorable acts was to inaugurate a dignified and demanding ceremony of initiation for Sikhs: it was called *khanda ka amrit*. In the presence of the Sikh Holy Book, five senior Sikh officials, *panch pyares*, kneel in a circle round a great bowl containing a sugar and water mixture, called *amrit*. The mixture is stirred steadily, with a sword—a great two-edged sword called a *khanda* (hence the name: *khanda ka amrit*). Prayers are said. The initiates come forward in turn and kneel. They are given some *amrit* to drink, a little *amrit* is sprinkled on their eyes, five times, and, again five times, *amrit* is sprinkled on their hair. As this happens, the officials call out:

'*Waheguru ji ka khalsa*'
('The Brotherhood is chosen by God')

and the candidates reply:

'*Waheguru ji ka fateh*'
('To God be the victory')

When all the candidates have come forward and
returned, they consume any *amrit* nectar that remains in
the bowl. They are then taught the great Sikh Prayer: the
Mool Mantra, and are put under vows to live the strict
Sikh way of life.

The honest sincerity of the Sikhs is well known, and it
is certain that the *amrit* ceremony has a great deal to do
with it. We need symbols and ceremonies: we are
ill-at-ease, confused and unhappy without them.
Greetings, hand-shakes, gestures and friendly phrases,
for instance, help to open up a conversation or make a
visitor feel at home.

Amrit has all the ingredients of a most effective
ceremony for the beginning of a rather special way of
life:

first, the *amrit* nectar itself, so carefully prepared, and
stirred with the sword, a symbol of survival and
determination, and yet the mixture is sweet to the taste;

secondly, the circle and the five *panch pyares*: a
suggestion of brotherhood: witness and friends;

thirdly, the threefold experience of the *amrit* nectar—by
taste, by sight (on the eyes) and by touch (on the
head)—an experience shared by all the candidates in
turn;

fourthly, the prayers, the presence of the Holy Book and
the vows;

fifthly, the friendly atmosphere over the refreshments
afterwards.

Spare a moment to recall the occasions when we find significance in the sharing of food and drink, when we find meaning in the meeting of important people to send the young on their way with a blessing. Can you call to mind any occasions when the western equivalent of the *amrit* nectar is applied to the eyes and the hair?

Here are some words from the *Mool Mantra*, which new Sikhs learn after *amrit*:

> '*Ekonkar*: There is one God
> His name is Eternal Truth.'

(The symbol is the *Gurmukhi* word '*Ekonkar*': There is one God.)

2

Chinese New Year

'The beginning of two weeks festivities to start the year' (January)

Symbol: The Yin and Yang symbol

Music: 'Peach Blossom Time', Side 2, Track 3 from 'The Chinese Violin', Candide CE 31037

In China, on the first day of the first lunar month, everyone starts the New Year Feast. Families are busy being happy at home, and visiting relatives.

Other things are important too: you try to pay off your debts and you buy a new set of clothes at this time. All manner of things help to spread the joy of New Year: peach and plum blossoms, chrysanthemums and daffodils, fruit and lanterns and sweets; and there are images of fish, often painted gold, to symbolise wealth. The Spirits are awakened and greeted with incense and firecrackers, children are given 'lucky coins' in red envelopes and everyone exchanges presents.

Fifteen days later, more lanterns—at home, in the temples, and in all the restaurants, and finally a great show of fireworks, with music.

It's the most natural thing in the world: to start the New Year with a bang. Did you? Did you 'see the Old Year out and the New Year in'? Did you sing 'Auld Lang Syne'? Do you know what it means? It's a song in praise of the good old times long since past—and, in another sense, the hope of good times still to come.

What strikes me about Chinese New Year is the joy of families together, surprises for the children, and visiting relatives. In British cities, by contrast, there were some lonely folk this New Year's Eve, the sick and elderly, the children left to make their own music whilst parents went to a party at another house. Perhaps most perplexing, because it is not untypical, there are many for whom the western Eve of New Year became an exercise in drinking to excess, and the first day of the New Year a hopeless non-event!

Recall a word from the opening remarks of this talk: *lunar*. Chinese New Year starts on the first day of the first lunar month. There are two particular thoughts about that. Here's the first.

Has it occurred to you to wonder why we have a seven day week? One theory is that our ancestors found the moon as mysterious as we do, in a simple, but more emotional way. They observed it closely, especially the full moon, as perhaps you do on a cloudless evening in spring or autumn. The moon is full every twenty-eight days, and the quarters come round every seven days. Men and women of many religions observe the moon with awe and reverence, and we have a lunar week! And, secondly: in some climates the moon is a safer bet than the sun! In the face of the seasonal upsets of nature that we seem to hear of so frequently now—drought and flood, crops lost and sheep and cattle hard to feed—it's a mighty miracle of nature that the seasons turn at all sometimes, and we have some sort of spring after winter, eventually, every year. Small wonder then that the monthly full face of the moon brings a kind of religious comfort, just because it is there: dependable, when all else seems unsure.

A great, ancient, wise teacher in China, Lao-Tse, taught that 'the way' to follow is, essentially, to be natural: to live as you were meant to, and these words from his teachings are very appropriate to our subject:

The way is like an empty jar.
You can draw water from it,
But it never needs to be filled.
The way has no beginning: it *is* the beginning:
The beginning of everything in the world.

3

The Beginning of Lent (Christian)

'Christians begin six weeks of prayer, study and self-denial in preparation for Easter' (February)

Symbol: The Cross

Music: Extract from Vaughan Williams' 'Antarctica'.

Lent begins on Ash Wednesday and ends on the day before Easter Sunday. It lasts about forty days. Jesus went off to be quietly by himself in the open and lonely hills by the Jordan for about forty days, when he knew for certain that his mission in life was to be the Son of God.

The two events: Jesus's six-week self-imposed exile and the six weeks of Lent, are closely connected in the minds of Christians, but for very different reasons. Church-going Christians especially Catholics, begin Lent with two days of serious self-examination. On Shrove Tuesday they examine their consciences, and many of them go to confession. They want to begin Lent with a 'clean sheet', as it were. 'Shrove' means 'forgiveness': they go to church to be 'shriven', a word that is related to the word 'script'—a document—a confession.

Then, on Ash Wednesday, many Christians go to Holy Communion, as they do on Sundays, but they leave church with ashes on their foreheads, as a mark of humility: 'Remember that from ashes you come and to ash you will return.' They are reminded that they are very human and easily tempted.

Maybe this is the link with Jesus, and his lonely meditation. At any rate, they spend the next six weeks or so under a voluntary 'rule of life'—more prayers, more church-going, charity-giving, going without things, self-denial. Jesus did without things too—but in his self-imposed exile he had no choice (except to go home again!)

If it is true that Jesus first fully understood his real identity and his mission in life when he went to John to be baptised, then clearly he needed time. He took a month-and-half. His lifework from then until his death was a mere three years. From his first day, by Galilee Lake he had clearly planned every move: he could foresee reaction, make decisions, and he never looked back. All the doubts were dealt with in the lonely hills of Jordan. Only one other moment of doubt is recorded: a moment that lasted three hours: on the eve of his death, in the Garden of Gethsemane.

By the Jordan Jesus faced, according to the story we know, three alternatives:

firstly, to use his 'special powers' (how familiar that phrase is now!)—to use these powers, not only to prevent him dying of hunger, thirst and exposure, but also to bring relief to the poor and needy of Palestine;

secondly, to confront the authorities with the mighty power of his Heavenly Father, in the Temple courtyard in Jerusalem: the very centre of Jewish and Roman power;

thirdly, to use his extraordinary personality to win people's friendship and loyalty.

He turned his back on each and everyone of these. He would bring help and healing in his own way in cases of emergency: indeed, people found these things simply by being with him. He would confront authority when there was no alternative. He would allow people to become his friends, but they must be absolutely free.

In fact, he would live naturally as a man of the people: but as a man with an unswerving mission. Apparently harmless and innocent, he would have a dynamic zest for truth and goodness. If this meant death, then so be it.

Christians, during Lent, think on these things. Death did come to Jesus, at Easter, and Christians, too, in a way, die and rise again with him through repentance and forgiveness.

4

Birthday of the Prophet (Muslim)

**'Muslims round the world celebrate the birthday of
the Prophet of Allah' (February)**

Symbol: Five-pointed Star of Islam

Music: 'Dervish Prayer', Side 2, Track 2 from 'Religions of the
Middle East', Argo ZFB 54 (start after flute solo).

We offer to all Muslims our greetings as they prepare to
celebrate the birthday of their Prophet, Muhammad
(peace be upon him).

Notice that when we mention the Prophet's name we
say 'peace be upon him'. Muslims are very particular
about their beliefs concerning the Prophet. They revere
him as the person who brought them the message of
God, which is enshrined forever in the Koran; but
they are quite insistent that he was a messenger and no
more than a messenger. When he died, it was said:
'Muhammad (peace be upon him) is dead, but God is
alive.'

But we should really start at the beginning. The
Prophet was born in the year AD 570, by our Western
calendar and Islam is quite young, as religions go—and
that makes its achievements all the more remarkable!

As a trader, Muhammad travelled, with his fellow
Arabs, from Mecca, west into Syria, where he is almost
certain to have met Jewish and Christian merchants.
After a while he married a rich widow and, with a little

time to spare, began to go away on his own to be quietly
by himself in prayer and meditation.

It was on one of these solitary journeys that he rested
in a cave on Mount Hira and became aware of a voice
commanding him to 'Recite'. After some hesitation he
did so and the words that came to him were a command
to preach one God only to the people of Mecca.

Naturally enough, he was at first still very hesitant,
but the 'visions' became a regular part of his life and he
eventually undertook the conversion of Mecca to the
pure faith of Allah, the One God. He was forty when
the first command came: and he was a man of immensely
strong personality. As it turned out, Mecca was not an
easy conquest and, with a group of friends and
followers, he retired to a place we now know as Medina.

That journey marked the turning point in his life: it
was as though the first Muslim community had been
born. The journey was called the *Hijra* and Muslims call
it the first Year of Islam: Year 1 AH. The community
grew and eight years later he returned to Mecca. His
reputation went before him and the people received him
without any opposition. Mecca became the centre of
Islam. The Prophet retired to Medina and died two years
later: in the year AD 632—or 11 AH.

At the festival of his birthday, hundreds of millions
of Muslims will remember Muhammad (peace be upon
him), and these words will be very much in their minds:

> In the name of God, most gracious, most merciful.
> Praise be to God, the Cherisher and Sustainer of the
>   Worlds;
> Most gracious, most merciful.
> Master of the day of judgement.
> Thee do we worship, and thine aid we seek.

5

Birthday of Ramakrishna (Hindu)

'The annual commemoration of a greatly-loved Hindu saint' (February)

Symbol: 'OM' symbol

Music: 'Dhun', Side 2, Track 1 from 'This is the Music of India', Philips 6460 854.

> 'You can get to the top of your house
> By using the stairs, or by climbing a ladder,
> By using a bamboo frame, or by climbing a rope.
> The ways to God are just as varied,
> And each religion has its own way.'

Those words were written by a remarkable Hindu saint who lived from 1836 to 1886. His name was Sri Ramakrsna Paramahamsa. He was born into a Brahmin, or priestly, Hindu family in Bengal and from an early age was quite evidently a naturally religious person with strong leanings towards meditation.

When he was twenty he became chief priest of a Kali Temple in Calcutta and his faith and devotion became gradually more intense. By modern, objective and critical standards, he would be described as eccentric, but his sweet nature so charmed those who met him that he gathered a substantial following. The very important Ramakrishna Vedanta Movement which flourishes today owes its existence to him, and to his disciple Swami Vivekenanda.

What particularly struck people about him was, first of all, his intense devotion: a real 'love' of the Goddess Kali combined with a strong 'intuition' about the nature of religion—and not only the Hindu religion.

This was the other, and perhaps eccentric, aspect of Ramakrishna: he was convinced that there is a Universal Truth in all religions. That is not so unusual—indeed it is a commonplace today to hear people say, 'all religions worship the same truth'. But Ramakrishna was prepared to go much further than that. He took up a practical interest in Islam: he dressed and lived like a Muslim and claimed to have had personal experience of Allah. He also spent some time living as a Christian and claimed to have had a personal experience of Jesus of Nazareth.

Questions come to mind: like 'How could he possibly actually believe in three different religions at once?' It would have been fascinating to have spoken with him: even more exciting to have introduced him in person in this talk. However, he did leave a wealth of writing which we can explore, for instance:

'When a mother has children who are ill,
She gives curry and rice to one,
Cereal with arrowroot to another,
And bread and butter to another.

In the same way, God has planned
Different kinds of religious practice for different people,
Each kind of religious practice designed
To suit each different personality.'

What is interesting is that he doesn't actually say that all regions are the same, in fact he seems to emphasise that religious traditions must be different: but within those differences there is a central truth—and that 'Truth' is that there is something 'Divine' in life.

Someone referred to him as being 'Full of Grace' and that is the impression we get of him too—it shows through his many poems. Here is another to end with:

> Bow your head and worship God,
> Where other people have knelt.
> The place where other people have offered God
> Their gift of adoration,
> These are the places where our gentle Lord
> Is bound to show himself,
> For he is kindness itself.

6

Mothering Sunday (Christian)

'The Family Festival of the Christian Churches' (March)

Symbol: The Cross

Music: Beginning of the 'Credo' from Beethoven's Missa Solemnis.

Consider the process by which a Christian family festival has become a commercial enterprise. Mothering Sunday was, originally, the day when Christians from young churches, mostly in country districts, came along to the mother church in the town, and celebrated a grand family reunion. At the same time, daughters might be able to visit their mothers (and bring their husbands, and perhaps a troop of children, to visit granny—with violets, and a special cake), and in the days when families had lots of daughters—often more than sons, this was some party!

And what do we have now, 'Mother's Day—complete with pricy cards, including VAT, pricy flowers, and all kinds of expensive suggestions for presents (or for making them yourself as on TV). And not content with that, we now have 'Father's Day', which has no foundation in history at all. And shops announce these events weeks in advance, just as they start the 'Back to School' syndrome at the very beginning of the holidays!

In the earliest days, gatherings of believers sprung up wherever the news of Jesus' life and death was taken, especially if the news was brought by an eye-witness. In some places, everything was written down, so that it could be checked when other men and women came with more news. We think that the gospel stories may have begun like this.

At any rate, as the numbers of believers increased (it was the Romans who first called them 'Christ-people', or Christians), so it became difficult for those in the country to travel in regularly to centres for worship, and village gatherings began. We would call them congregations or assemblies, but the word 'church' was adopted. It now means two things: first, the Lord's House, and secondly, all the people in it.

Things haven't changed very much down the years: the New Testament is full of curiously charming touches about the business of looking after all the churches. In one of his letters Paul says that in spite of being put in prison, beaten, and shipwrecked, he still firmly believed that his hardest job was looking after all the churches. We hear about one church where in-fighting was common: Paul gave them some strong advice about loving each other—which has come down to us as a kind of 'Ode to Charity', the last words of which are 'so there are faith, hope and charity, but the greatest is charity'. It's good now and then to see these magnificent passages in their original contexts. Some other Christians apparently forgot themselves at Communion: in those days Holy Communion was a real meal with the service as it is known today in the middle. These people, in Paul's letter, couldn't wait to get at the food—and the wine—and by the time everyone had arrived, some of the first arrivals had had rather too much to drink! And there are some delightful descriptions of churches in Asia Minor (now Turkey): one of them was so lukewarm—so lazy—that it made the Bishop feel sick (or so he said). By the way, the word 'bishop' comes from a word that means 'Inspector'—an interesting idea: an 'Inspector of Churches'!

Once a year the Bishop gathered all his flock together, and they came, in their enormous family groups for a grand family service. That's what Mothering Sunday is about. But that's no reason why you shouldn't give your mother a card, some flowers, and a present—home-made, like those you may have seen on TV.

7

Purim (Jewish)

'In a mood of high carnival, Jews remember Esther, whose beauty and courage saved her people from disaster' (March)

Symbol: Six-pointed Star of David

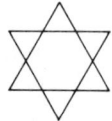

Music: 'Song of a Wayfarer', Side 1, Track 6 from 'Esther Ofarim: Israeli Songs', Columbia SCX 6297.

At Purim, there is excitement, stamping and shouting in Jewish houses and synagogues. In Israel there are carnival processions and fancy-dress parades—and all because of a pretty girl called Esther, who became Queen of Persia, and advised the King of Persia, just in time to save her people from wholesale massacre.

It all happened many centuries ago in Susa, the capital of Persia. The King staged a great banquet, but his Persian wife Vashti rather spoiled things by refusing to attend. There were lots of Jewish people living in Susa and a young Jewess called Esther agreed to take her place.

One of the King's chief ministers, called Haman, had taken a dislike to Esther's uncle, and had conceived a plot to exterminate the Jewish population. But he had not reckoned with Esther. She used her privileged position to leak the news to the King and he was furious. He had Haman executed. The Jews celebrated in the streets of Susa and have done so everywhere ever since.

Everyone listens to the story of Esther, in the synagogue, with a mixture of pride and amusement, specially the children. Whenever Haman's name is mentioned, they have official permission to stamp and shout in triumphant mockery of his ill-starred plot and Esther's clever counter-plan.

Haman used 'lots' (a system of random choice, like throwing a dice, or tossing a coin) to choose the day of the massacre: little did he know that the lot would fall on his own head—the idea caught on, and Jews called the Festival 'Lots' or *Purim*.

The Jews must be the world's oldest group of 'immigrants', and yet they have a happy knack of making happy homes wherever they are, and becoming natural, and often leading citizens of their towns and cities. Apparently, Susa was no exception, and Esther quickly made herself at home in the palace! Spare a thought, for the large numbers of members of other faiths and cultures whom we take for granted, but would miss very much if they suddenly betook themselves home.

And it's right that the Jews should be proud of their history, and celebrate occasions like Esther's undercover counter plot. The Jews have so many tragic memories, it's good to join them in the carefree carnival spirit of Purim. It's likely there'll be all-night Hora-dancing (lively dancing in circles) in the towns and villages of new Palestine and the story will be told over again, with relish:

All the city of Susa shouted for joy. For the Jews there was light and joy, gladness and honour . . . feasting and holiday . . .

Praise the Lord, all nations: Praise Him, all peoples: For his loving kindness is powerful for us. His truth endures for ever.

8

Holi (Hindu)

'Hindus the world over are in carnival mood in honour of Lord Krishna' (March)

Symbol: 'OM' symbol

Music: 'Krishna, Krishna', Side 2, Track 2 from 'Ravi Shankar's Music Festival from India', Dark Horse Records AMLH 22007 (A & M Records). (Where the vocal part starts).

Hindus around the world celebrate Holi—the festival of Lord Krishna, the Hindu Spring Festival, the 'festival of colours', the festival of love—so many things to celebrate at once! But Hindus don't mind—to them, many things are one thing and one thing many things.

Lord Krishna is the favourite of Hindus everywhere. He is the earthly form of the God Vishnu, whose divine energy supports the life of the universe. In his earthly form, Krishna represents, among many things, that quality that we all recognise as the basic quality of life: warm, kind and tender *love*.

We have a saying from a poem by Tennyson: 'In the spring a young man's fancy lightly turns to thoughts of love'. All the great religions. have an exciting, happy, sometimes wildly playful festival in the spring. It is as though religion recognises the awakening of Nature—or perhaps that religion *is* Nature!

At any rate, Krishna is remembered in the spring as the enchanting young man who stole the hearts of all the girls in old India, especially in his traditional home village of Vrindaban. He married the beautiful Radha, and young Hindus still seek his blessing on their love-life and ask his help in finding a good husband or a pretty wife.

Lord Krishna's popularity was not one little bit spoiled by stories about him teasing people and playing tricks on them! Indeed, Hindus seem to like him all the more for that and they pretend to beat him at his own game at the Holi festival! If you're ever invited to Holi, don't wear your best clothes: it's carnival time, and everyone is carrying red or violet powder or water-solution. The idea is to splash the bright colour on as many fellow Hindus as possible, and if you come home covered with colour-stains, you reckon you've thoroughly enjoyed yourself, and had a very good festival!

You could call it 'spring fever'!—and maybe, like so many spring festivals, it goes back into the ancient mists of the celebration of new love in the dawn of Nature's year.

In Vrindaban, Krishna's home and the centre of millions of annual Krishna pilgrimages, Holi lasts a week!

Our friends from the East are, predictably, always sad and sorry that spring in Britain is so often 'a little late', and Holi does not always fall on a beautifully warm spring day! But, not surprisingly, Hindu spirits are not dampened by rain, frost or even a little late snow: Krishna's attractive qualities are warmer than the weather! Hindus put it this way:

'Krishna said:
"Think on Me: love Me: devote yourself to Me;
Offer Me your gifts: your adoration;
This is how you can come to Me: this I promise you:
Indeed I do: for you are dear to Me." '

(*Bhagavad Gita*: 18.65/66)

9

Easter (Christian)

'Christians celebrate the Death and Resurrection of Jesus Christ' (April)

Symbol: The Cross

Music: 'Resurrexit' from Bach's B Minor Mass.

To be quite correct we should not think about the events of the first Easter Sunday until the day arrives, but since it is usual to celebrate all the events of Easter together, at least at school, we should begin by listing the ones that matter—the ones that can be included in a five-minute talk.

Jesus knew that he would meet a violent death: it was the only possible outcome of his life of quiet but insistent preaching of truth, self-discipline, and sincere worship of God. These were things that ordinary people could understand, but were an embarrassment to the authorities, who were the victims of their own history. He was also a personal embarrassment to the Roman powers in Palestine: they saw him as a popular leader and a potential threat to peace.

On Palm Sunday he made these feelings public by riding openly into Jerusalem and allowing himself to be greeted as 'the one who comes in the Name of the Lord'.

On the Thursday of the same week, about eighteen hours before his death, he gathered his disciples for the customary meal together before Passover and begged them to remember him at future meals. He shared bread and wine with them and invited them to see the sharing as a kind of giving of himself to them.

Judas left to arrange for Jesus' arrest and Jesus left for the garden where he often went to pray. To many devout Christians, it was in the garden that Jesus, in the deepest agony of the human heart, faced the choice of everyman: whether to save himself or to allow events to kill him. His decision was to do neither of these things, but simply to surrender himself to his Father's wish. From that moment, events have the air of finality: Jesus endured them, but was never in doubt about taking any other course.

There are no grounds for any doubt about the events that followed: his arrest in the garden, his trials before the Jewish and Roman authorities, the beating to secure a confession and the crucifixion, naked in the heat of the day and in full view of a wholly insolent crowd, apart from his devoted and closest friends and, of course, his mother and Mary Magdalene.

It is more than likely that he died quite soon. The piercing of the body with a spear would be to convince the unbelieving women that he was indeed dead.

About the burial there is room for doubt. Maybe he was taken to burial sepulchre nearby for the time being, perhaps one of a number grouped together. Certainly this might explain how two of the disciples might have visited the wrong sepulchre and found it empty, with the stone at the entrance still in the open position.

What is impossible to explain away is the quite extraordinary change of heart on the part of the disciples and friends some thirty-six hours later. They had been quite downcast and without hope and yet within a very short time they were together again and beginning to tell everyone that he (Jesus) was 'risen'—back among them. Their joy, their energy and their conviction can only be explained by some experience—possibly many experiences—of his real personal presence: as though he had 'risen from the dead'.

The day he died was Passover day. Just as the Passover lambs, by their blood, had saved the Jews from Egypt in the Old Testament story, so Jesus' death is believed to be God's way of saving man—from himself.

10

Pesach (Jewish)

'Every year at this time Jews recall their deliverance from slavery under Pharoah and their birth, under Moses, as the people of Yahweh' (April)

Symbol: Six-pointed Star of David

Music: 'Shema Israel', Side 1, Track 1 from 'Music From Israel', Argo ZFB 50.

The Passover (Pesach) is such an important festival for Jewish people, that it is easy to forget just how many aspects of Judaism are commemorated at this time.

Above all, Passover celebrates escape. Under the leadership of Moses and the guidance of Yahweh (God), the Jews left Egypt and began life as a nation in their own right. It was also the beginning of the Jewish Faith, and of their journey to their promised home in Israel.

But it's also the Jewish Festival of Spring, and, in a way, of spring-cleaning too. To take one example: houses were (and still are) thoroughly cleaned. Old barley yeast is disposed of, and, in the old days, barley bread was made without yeast until the new barley yeast was ready: that's why they eat unleavened bread, or *matzoth* at the festival.

The escape from Egypt (about 3,200 years ago) coincided with the Spring Barley Festival, and the two have been closely linked ever since. The Passover meal is eaten round the table, at home, with all the family present, and the story of the escape is told over again, with the children asking questions and learning the meaning of the *matzoth* and the bitter herbs. It's interesting how religion and Nature so often seem so close. Spring festivals, with religious and natural significance crowd into the calendar at this time of the year.

But this one is very much about God in action. It was God who planned the escape: God who masterminded it: God who made it possible: and God who showed himself to the people as they made their journey out of Egypt with Moses.

In fact, it was a revelation which would not take 'No' for an answer—the revelation of 'God to the rescue'. As a Jew, you learn about God not so much by what he is as by what he does. He says: 'I am the Lord thy God who brought you out of the Land of Egypt.'

The story is full of the wonder of the acts of God: the night of the Passover itself, the parting of the waters, the light and the cloud to guide the people to Sinai.

In fact, there might have been just the hint that the Jews 'had it made', that they were 'spoonfed with salvation'—but it was not by any means the case. At Sinai the people learned how they were expected to keep their part of the 'salvation bargain' by following God's commandments. 'Thou shalt' and 'Thou shalt not' were very much the order of the day. That covenant or agreement has a festival all to itself, later in the year.

As the Passover begins, Jews will pray these words:

> Thou hast given us in love, O Lord our God,
> Appointed times for gladness, festivals and
>   seasons of joy;
> This day of the Feast of Unleavened Bread,
> The season of our Freedom.

11

The Birthday of Shakyamuni (Buddhist)

'Buddhists recall, with affection, the birth of their Founder' (April)

Symbol: The Wheel of Life

Music: 'Haru No Umi', Side 1, Track 2 from 'Japanese Koto Music', Lyrichord LLST 7131.

Someone said quite recently that, whilst in general, organised religion in this country seems to be on the decline, some religious groups in the United Kingdom are steadily increasing in numbers. For instance, it is reported that the number of Buddhists here is growing steadily.

The Buddha was born in India in 563 BC. He left his rich home and family and sought the cause of suffering. He rejected the hard life of a wandering holy man, and after a long period of intense meditation, found the answer to suffering in the complete transformation of every person's attitude to life, to suffering and to himself. But it is the young Buddha: under his birth name of Siddartha Gautama that everyone is thinking about—especially in Japan, where there are nearly 50 million Buddhists and a temple in every town.

The temples have pleasant gardens and elegant fishpools. On the Buddha's birthday, children put on beautiful gold-embroidered costumes, often handed down through the family. They carry lotus blossoms made of paper to the temples. Inside, the image of the young Gautama is covered in pink flowers: the devotees bow in reverence before the shrine.

Then something happens which is very strange to us, but on second thoughts very typical of the East: each devotee carefully pours over the head of the image a small amount of sweet hydrangea tea. The reason? A Japanese legend says that on the day of Gautama's birth it rained sweet hydrangea tea.

Does all this seem too curious? Too exotic? Do you wonder at all the attention that they give to a baby? There are many legends about the young Gautama, for instance, that the unborn Buddha child entered the mother in the guise of a superb pure white elephant; that this event turned out to be a dream, and that he was born after ten months in the womb; that he was born already able to stand, and that he walked immediately, saying, 'I shall lead the world'. But stories like these are the fruit of centuries of devotion. And, speaking of Holy Children: what would Christmas be like without the stories about the stable, the shepherds and the wise men, the angels, the donkey, and 'gold, frankincense and myrrh'?

This is a Buddhist prayer:

No altar fires for me: no wood for sacrifices,—the fire I light is right inside myself, burning bright and warm. My life is the sacrifice, my heart is the altar, for I am a disciple of the Buddha.

12

Baisakhi (Sikh)

**'Birthday of a Brotherhood: Sikhs remember the
founding of the Khalsa' (April)**

Symbol: The Sword Symbol

Music: 'Duhn', Side 2, Track 1 from 'This is the Music of
India', Philips 6460 854.

At this time Sikh communities nationwide, along with
Sikhs throughout the world, are remembering a strange
event, an important person and their own religious
family tree.

It was Guru Nanak, who forged a magnificently
simple and courageous new faith for the people of the
Punjab in the sixteenth century. The early days for the
new community of Sikhs were not easy, and the first ten
leaders, or *gurus*, worked without rest, often sacrificing
their lives, until the time came for the Sikhs to recognise
themselves and their beliefs as independent, sincere and
enduring.

That time came in 1699, on the occasion of a festival
called *Baisakhi*. The Sikhs came together for prayer and
praise at Anandpur, always with a lingering fear of the
invading Mogul armies. Guru Gobind Rai, their leader,
the tenth *Guru*, suddenly drew his sword and demanded
'the head of a Sikh'.

Everyone was horrified, but at last a man stepped
forward, saying 'My head is at your service'. Gobind Rai
took him into his tent and reappeared, dripping sword

in hand. 'Another head,' he cried. The strange, appalling performance continued until five men had offered themselves. Then at last, Gobind Rai brought the five heroes out unharmed for everyone to see and also the carcass of a goat.

So the *Khalsa* began: a brotherhood of five men, all of them ready to offer themselves in sacrifice for the Truth, for God whose name is Truth; they are pure, and brothers in faith. Gobind Rai gave them the name *'Singh'* (lion), and joined the Khalsa himself. Other men joined, and women too: (a woman was called *Kaur*: princess). Admission to the Khalsa was then, and is still today, considered a very serious matter: the ceremony is called *Amrit*.

Members of the Khalsa today are distinguished by wearing their hair long and tied up under a turban. To us it seems a specially courageous thing to do: to wear a turban continually because of your religion. It depends how you view your religion. If religion is a Sunday speciality, then on Monday and Tuesday and the rest, it becomes a habit to put religious observances aside. How many of us still say 'Grace' at meals, or say prayers morning and night as a family? But if, like a Sikh, your religion *is* your life, then every step in the street is before God: and the turban is worn for him.

And Baisakhi is for him: they sing in praise of God and in reverence for Guru Nanak and Guru Gobind Singh in words such as these:

> There is only one God.
> His name is 'True', for he *is* true,
> And all truth comes from him.
> He was not born, and will not die:
> He is life itself.

13

Wesak (Buddhist)

'Buddhists celebrate the life and work of their founder, Gautama the Buddha' (May)

Symbol: Wheel of Life

Music: 'Haru No Umi', Side 1, Track 2 from 'Japanese Koto Music', Lyrichord LLST 7131.

On the night of the full moon in May Buddhists keep *Wesak*. They decorate their homes, arrange rows of lighted candles, give presents and hold processions. Wesak is the day when Buddhists celebrate the birth, the enlightenment and the death of their founder, Siddartha Gautama.

There are many stories about the Buddha: about the way he turned his back on his luxurious home, and how after long journeys and much heart-searching, he found the answer to the suffering of mankind and devoted the rest of his long life to sharing his secret with the people of India.

The secret referred to: the secret which attracted so many followers, and has made Buddhism one of the world's great religions—one that is still growing fast—the secret is exactly what it says, a secret! It's meaning is at once so simple and so profound that most of us cannot grasp it, let alone live by it, at least to begin with. To understand it requires not so much a mental effort, as a personal surrender. It's really a question of waiting until your mind has stopped rushing about from this thought to that and is at peace. Then you must wait again, until you have found a kind of emotional tranquillity—and at the same time, there should be a physical quietness in the body. Then the secret is plain. It can best be appreciated by that part of you that enjoys a radiant sunset, a piece of great music, or a rare example of a mountain landscape—your personal intuition—inner experience. In that moment of hushed awareness, the secret is clear: for the secret *is* the awareness—a mighty 'stepping-back' to view life as it should be seen: not from the midst of the wretched routine of every day, but from a personal mood of collected thoughts.

This is not a retreat from reality, an escape from daily life. Indeed, the Buddhist brings this mood of detachment to the labours of his own life—whether as a manual worker, a teacher, a housewife or a monk, and performs those labours more efficiently and with less fatigue. But there is more to come.

In celebrating the Buddha's 'death', Buddhists are remembering something which is very different from the kind of death that we are familiar with. They call it *parinibbana*. All through life man can experience moments of stillness—a kind of living *nibbana*: but when the body slips away, the 'stillness' remains: the *nibbana* is complete—and best called *parinibbana*—the 'stillness' lives on by itself! Not an easy idea to understand, but it *is* a 'secret' and the Buddha himself did not find it easy.

At Wesak, Buddhists think about the end of their Founder's earthly life. These words are taken from the story of his last hours on earth:

The Buddha said, 'The time for my entry into *Nibbana* has now arrived. These are my last words.' . . . The earth quivered like a ship struck by a squall . . . the moon's light waned . . . an uncanny darkness spread everywhere . . . trees nearby bent their boughs over him and showered his body with flowers.

14

The Martyrdom of Guru Arjan Dev (Sikh)

'Sikhs remember Guru Arjan Dev, who built the Golden Temple at Amritsar' (May)

Symbol: The Sword Symbol

Music: 'Dhun', Side 2, Track 1 from 'This is the Music of India', Philips 6460 854.

It must be a rare privilege to look down on the Golden Temple of Amritsar at festival time. Added to the beauty of the temple itself, festooned with thousands of festival lights, is the reflection of the whole brilliant panorama in the waters of the lake that completely surrounds the building. This description is an eloquent tribute to the memory of Guru Arjan Dev Singh, who built it. In May Sikhs around the world remember him and his martyrdom again: a Sikh in the true tradition, who gave his life for his faith some 370 years ago. The Sikhs remember the stories about the rigours of the early years of the Sikh tradition. Arjan Dev contributed to the enduring faith of his people in two ways: building the temple and compiling the first part of the Sikh Holy Book.

The temple is a living lesson in Sikh attitudes to life. First: any person may enter the temple, by any door. Sikhs contend that all men and women are equal in the sight of God. God is Truth, and the only differences between men are those they make themselves: that is:

the degrees to which men differ in their willingness to accept the Truth.

Second: all the entrances to the temple involve going downstairs. You cannot look up to God until you have first stepped down to the foundation of man's life: a modest humility.

Thirdly: like all Sikh temples, or *gurdwaras*, a vital part of the building is the *langar*, or community room, where all-comers may take refreshment. Clearly, at the time of its building, Sikhs badly needed an identity of their own, a place to call their Holy House and somewhere to meet and converse with friends and feed travellers. But the need of the moment became an article of faith.

Arjan Dev also compiled the *Adi-Granth*—the first part of the Sikh Holy Book: the *Guru Granth Sahib.* In every *gurdwara* it is the Holy Book which is the focal point of attention. Constantly attended by a member of the congregation, who waves to and fro a slender emblem of the authority of the book, the words of the *Granth Sahib* themselves provide the faithful with the words of their worship and the words of their inspiration for everyday life. And it was Arjan Dev who conceived the notion of compiling the Book: a gathering of the wisdom of Guru Nanak, the founder, and of the poems and prayers of other holy men.

His work, not only for the Faith, but also for the welfare of his people, by way of trade and industry, gave him the reputation of being a popular hero—which of course he was; but it made him something of a threat to the rulers of his day and he received a martyr's death.

Arjan's collection was meant to be sung, but the following words make their point just as well in the spoken voice:

> As waves beating on the shingle,
> Go back and mingle in the ocean,
> So from God came all things under the sun:
> And return to God when their race is run.

15

The Ascension of Bahá'u'lláh (Bahá'í)

'The Passing of the Great Teacher of the Bahá'í Faith' (May)

Symbol: Nine-pointed Star

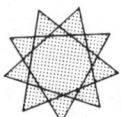

Music: 'Duhn', Side 2, Track 1 from 'This is the Music of India', Philips 6460 854.

The teachings of the Bahá'í Faith are to be found in the writings of Bahá'u'lláh. The name means 'Glory of God' and he proclaimed himself 'The Promised One of God' in 1863. He was a Persian, born in 1817, and he could have had a bright career as a government officer. But he chose instead to involve himself in charity work, found himself in the middle of a political hassle and was put in prison. There, in deprivation and indignity, he found God. However, his beliefs and his teaching were not at all acceptable in Persia and he began a succession of imprisonments and exiles, until at last he arrived at Akka, on the coast of Palestine. For twenty-four years he lived on, still under substantial restrictions.

But his ministry in Akka was charismatic: he seemed to radiate love where all had been hatred and persecution. It was as though he had brought a new spirit of life to mankind. After his death in 1892, those who followed his teaching—we call them Baha'is continued to proclaim the truth of his claim to be 'The Promised One'. He is believed to rank with Jesus, Moses and Muhammad, as a prophet of the Universal God.

Wherever nine persons (or more than nine) come together with a common acceptance of the Bahá`í Faith, there is an 'Assembly'.

Bahá`ís claim that Bahú`u`lláh is the final prophet of God, and that his message is Universal. God, they say, shows himself to men as and when they are ready to receive him. Way back in history, Moses revealed him to the Hebrews, and after Moses, the Buddha and Zoroaster—in the sixth century BC. Then, later, Jesus of Nazareth, and Muhammad—and most recently—just over 100 years ago, Bahá`u`lláh: and he is to be the last. His revelation is complete, and sufficient in itself for the modern world.

Naturally, Bahá`ís have strong feelings about marriage, about death and about the proper way to live. They are also, understandably, most particular about preserving the words of their teacher. The closing words are taken from the writings of Bahá`u`lláh:

This is a matchless day. Matchless must, likewise, be the tongue that celebrateth the praise of the desire of all nations . . . the whole human race hath longed for this day, that perchance it may fulfil that which well beseemeth its station, and is worthy of its destiny. Blessed is the man whom the affairs of the world have failed to deter from recognising him who is the Lord of all things.

(*Writings of Baha-u-llah* XVI).

Most religions prophesy about a day of judgement and righteousness of heaven on earth. Bahá`u`lláh claims that his coming fulfils these· prophecies, and the new teachings from God for this age will bring about the long-awaited 'most great peace'.

16

Whitsun (Christian)

'Christians celebrate the birthday of the Church'
(May)

Symbol: The Cross

Music: 'Veni Sancte Spiritus' (Plainsong).

Whitsunday, like Easter, changes its date every year. This is because both festivals are closely linked with the Jewish calendar, and this in turn is governed by the moon and the spring equinox. This need not worry anybody—and, as a matter of fact, we now have a separate Spring Bank Holiday which is more or less fixed, and people have largely forgotten what Whitsunday or Whitsun or even 'Whit' is all about!

The 'Whit' bit is quite simply short for 'White': the day was originally known as *White Sunday*. It falls on the fiftieth day after Easter—and for that reason sometimes has the Greek name Pentecost meaning fiftieth day. Early Christian converts seeking to join the Church would come dressed in white on Whitsunday, to be baptised and receive Holy Communion. They spent a fair time prior to the great day in rigorous preparation, and were usually brought into church by their sponsor (just as often still happens with young people, for confirmation of first Communion).

The choice of Whitsunday for this occasion was probably due to the events which are reported to have taken place on the first Pentecost day. Jesus's family, friends and disciples were meeting together, when something quite extraordinary happened. It was as though a great surge of energy pervaded the room. Everyone felt it, and Luke, describing it many years later, says that there appeared on them 'tongues of fire'. They all began chattering with the excitement of the moment, and people in the street outside couldn't make up their minds what was going on: some said that they heard people in the room speaking in foreign languages: others said it was a drunken party.

Anyway, the upshot was that Peter, now the leader, by common consent (a fascinating about-face for the man who disowned Jesus at his trial), announced that the event was the fulfillment of an old promise, that the Lord's Spirit would be with his people. He gave it as his considered belief that the work that Jesus had begun should now continue: that those who believed that Jesus was the Son of God (the Messiah, the Christ) should come forward and be baptised. The response was enormous: people came in their thousands and this must have kept the disciples busy for some considerable time.

And that is how the Christian Church began. just as Christmas is the birthday of Jesus, so Whitsunday is the birthday of the Church. From that day, the people of Christ (the Romans called them Christ-people, or *Christians*), travelled through the lands of the Eastern Mediterranean, as far as Rome, with a simple message: that Jesus went about doing good, and healing the sick; that he was arrested by Pilate, tried, crucified, dead and buried; that he rose from the dead; that he reigns over the world; and that he will return. This was the message that in turn gave rise to the first written documents about Jesus and eventually to the Gospels.

People today often go away for Whit, and this is right and proper. But it's also right and proper to spare a thought for the high spirits in the big front room upstairs, in about AD 28, which set the Christian Church off on its 2,000 years of history.

17

Trinity Sunday (Christian)

**'Christians renew their faith in the Holy Trinity'
(June)**

Symbol: The Cross

Music: 'Sanctus' from Verdi's Requiem.

The word *Trinity* is familiar enough in Christian connections: we hear it in names such as Trinity College, Holy Trinity Church and Trinity Sunday. In fact in the Christian calendar, there are about twenty-five Sundays named after the Trinity: that's nearly half the year: from just after Whitsun to about a month before Christmas.

The word gets borrowed by other people too—every rugby player has heard of Wakefield Trinity and sometimes a group of three important people is referred to as a 'trinity'. And that's a clue to its meaning. Literally it means 'threeness'.

But it's not really a Bible word at all and doesn't appear there anywhere. The earliest Christians began to use the word when they were talking about 'God the Father, God the Son and God the Holy Ghost'. And that's where the trouble starts. You don't have to be a Christian to know that God, in Christian belief is not actually anyone's father, in the usual meaning of the word anyway. And he's not anyone's son either: how could he be? And he's certainly not a Ghost, especially a Holy one!

So what do Christians mean when they use the word, either in a prayer, or perhaps in the hymn that starts 'Holy, Holy, Holy, Lord God Almighty' where each verse ends with the words 'blessed Trinity'?

The problem is that we are trying to use ordinary human words to describe ideas that we cannot understand, really properly. God is, in a very important, but a puzzling kind of way, the Creator of the universe. At the same time, he keeps the universe alive. In fact, the universe draws its life from him and he is present in every little part of it. Now the best word, from our human experience, to describe him doing all these things, is *Father*, but please remember that some ancient religious traditions prefer to think of a female God figure (rather like 'Mother Earth')—but try suggesting that Christians should start believing in God the Mother! Our parents were responsible for creating us, they helped us to grow up strong and healthy and they live on in each of us (we call it 'heredity'), so you can see why God the Father is about the best description.

What about God the Son? The Christmas and Easter stories are about Jesus of Nazareth. A great deal of mystery surrounds his birth, his death and his resurrection, and that's because Jesus is believed to be quite unique: completely human, but at the same time completely God. He is often called 'Son of God' and, when you think about it, there's probably no better way of describing him. 'Son' is a word that really means: very closely related, having his father's characteristics, and, above all, *loving* his father and being *loved* by him. This is how Jesus was: so close to God that people found it easy to believe that, although he was so completely and superbly human, he really was God, all the time.

And as regards the 'Holy Ghost' we can do no better than consider an idea which makes it much easier to understand. The word 'ghost', like 'spirit', means 'life' without a body to live in. The life that God shared with Jesus and, even more so, their *love* for each other, is the power that binds Christians to God as well, and to each other. So the Holy Ghost, or Holy Spirit, is real and all three members of the Trinity are ways we think of God at work. They may be three 'persons' as we say, but there is only one God in the end.

18

Shavuot (Jewish)

'At Shavuot, or Pentecost, Jews remember the giving of the Law to Moses' (June)

Symbol: Six-pointed Star of David

Music: 'Shema Israel', Side 1, Track 1 from 'Music from Israel', Argo ZFB 50.

On the fiftieth day (Pentecost Day) after Passover, Jews remember how Moses received the Ten Commandments from God (Yahweh as they call him) on Mount Sinai. According to the Bible and the Calendar of the Jewish Year, the events on Mount Sinai happened just seven weeks after the great escape from Egypt. That escape was very much the gracious act of God. The Israelites' part in the plan was simply to do as Moses told them. But some two months later the scene is set for the completion of the agreement, or Covenant as the Jews call it.

God tells Moses: 'I am the Lord your God, who brought you out of the land of Egypt' and then, immediately, the response of the people is required in no uncertain terms: 'You must have no other Gods before me.'

God's powerful act demands the people's exclusive faith: *No other God but Yahweh.*

It is almost as though God is saying 'You have met gods already, in Egypt, and you will meet others. But remember: *I am your God*—the one who brought you out of Egypt'.

What follows are a number of rules about various aspects of life: about thoughtful worship, setting aside one day a week for God, careful and loving family life, and the keeping of simple social rules which would be essential if they were to reach the Holy Land safely.

Every year, Jews renew their vows to keep the Commandments. But there's more to it than just the Commandments. What Moses received on the Holy Mountain was the *Torah—the whole Law*: the whole story of God's plan for his people, and their faith in him. Jews profess their trust in the whole story—in God's continuing powerful love for his people and their need for his help.

Shavuot is a favourite time of year for *Bar-Mitzvah* ceremonies: young men and women in their early teens undergo a ceremony of becoming 'Sons and Daughters of the Law'. Chanting of the Holy Scriptures is involved and those who participate are then deemed to be full members of the Jewish community, of the synagogue, and of the family. Everyone knows that at that precise time when most young people seem to be straining for an identity and a culture which is (or seems to be) utterly different from the experience and the values of their parents, Jewish young people vow themselves into closer conformity and do so with pride.

These words are taken from the story of Moses on Mount Sinai: (God is speaking):

> Take these words of mine to heart: . . .
> Teach them to your children,
> Mention them when you are sitting at home,
> Mention them when you are out walking,
> Write them down . . . .
> Keep them in the forefront of your mind.
> Write them on the front door post.
> Write them on the gateway.

19

Rath Yatra (Hindu)

'Hindus draw huge temples on wheels through the streets, in honour of Lord Jagannath' (June)

Symbol: 'OM' symbol

Music: 'Dhun', Side 2, Track 1 from 'This is the Music of India', Philips 6460 854. (Use the rhythmic, march-like section.)

Sometimes when people want to make a public announcement about the way they feel about something, they not only have a meeting about it, but often organise a procession through the streets. One of the most famous processions in India, and among some groups of Hindus in this country, is *Rath Yatra*—the festival of Lord Jagannath.

We owe more to Lord Jagannath than we are aware of! We use his very name to describe the monster lorries that eat up our motorways—'Juggernauts'. And that is the clue to the Rath Yatra Festival: Lord Jagannath is drawn through the streets on a huge chariot: a kind of 'temple on wheels'. In case you should think there is something unusual, or irrational, about taking God for a walk, consider for a moment the way Jewish people carry their scriptures round the synagogue and how Christians carry the Virgin Mary round the towns in Spain. Taking God for a walk is the natural thing to do, in many countries and among many cultures.

But what has that got to do with us? A very great deal. Imagine the reactions of Hindus to the approach of

Jagannath's chariot: God is coming down the High Street, round the corner and up *your* street. You are thankful that you have your best clothes on and are fit to be seen by him. Your house is neat and tidy: fit for Jagannath to pass by. You sing, you pray, you laugh and you dance, in his honour.

In many ways our Western culture is sophisticated—perhaps too much so. For us, everything is 'in the mind'—rationalised out of existence. Most of us—even the religious ones—would be too shy to take part in a religious procession. Most of us would be inclined to say, 'I try to live at peace with my neighbour: and do some good when I can'—and that's quite a respectable religious outlook, probably based on the idea that we are all the 'children of God'. (Whether you actually believe in a God or worship God, or not.)

But there is one other point: so alright, we don't carry crucifixes in procession like they used to, and the few Christians who still regularly go 'on parade' are our good friends, the Salvation Army. But there *are* two common religious processions you can see any day of the week—and like Jagannath, they are on wheels. When you see a funeral procession, do you pause a moment, in the face of every man's destiny? When you see a wedding car, white streamers fluttering, do you pause to wish them well?

Here are some words of Hindu praise:

> Homage to the Breath of Life, for this whole
>   Universe obeys Him . . .
> O Breath of Life: turn not your back on me:
>   For you are none other than myself . . .
> As droplets in a pool of water,
>   So within myself do I enclose you
> Else I cannot live, without you.

(Artha Veda)

20

Dhamma Vijaya (Buddhist)

'Buddhists celebrate the spread of their beliefs throughout the world' (June)

Symbol: The Wheel of Life

Music: 'Haru no Umi', Side 1, Track 2 from 'Japanese Koto Music', Lyrichord LLST 7131.

After the death of the Buddha, five centuries before the birth of Jesus, Buddhist teaching about the purpose of life, the nature of man, the origin of suffering and its cure, was widely known and respected in India. And so it remained, for 200 years. And then came the Emperor Ashoka, who was crowned in 265 BC. His experience of war, of suffering, violence and senseless slaughter led him to a vow never again to engage in a war. He became a Buddhist and actively encouraged the spread of Buddhist teaching.

He made it an offence not only to take human life, but also to kill animals. He provided all manner of help for those who were sick or homeless or without water, or shelter from the hot sun. He sent Buddhist missionaries out to spread the teaching of the Buddha, and set up local communities. To help with this, he made the teaching simple and attractive for people to understand and built temples for everyone to visit every week.

The effect of his work is still quite evident—there are

strong Buddhist communities in Sri Lanka, Burma, Thailand, Cambodia and Laos. And these early missionary activities led to the spread of Buddhism to China and Japan.

Why was Ashoka so successful? Certainly he seemed to have the gift of strong leadership without which nothing could have been achieved. But his understanding of Buddhism itself was not only true to the faith, but it was simple. He spoke frequently of the central importance of the Buddha himself, the teaching (*Dhamma*), and the close Buddhist community of monks and nuns. But probably it was the teaching itself that appealed to the people everywhere and certainly it is the spread of that teaching, the *Dhamma Vijaya*, that the Buddhist communities remember with affection in June.

Here are the five foundations of that *Dhamma* or teaching:
(1) you must not take life;
(2) you must not take what is not given to you;
(3) you must not be unfaithful in marriage;
(4) you must not tell a lie;
(5) you must not take alcohol.

You must understand, of course, that you do not become a Buddhist just by keeping these rules, but it is worthy of your consideration to note that if a Buddhist came to visit you, you would find that he was:
(1) a vegetarian;
(2) politely hesitant about accepting hospitality;
(3) easily embarrassed by sexy jokes and swearing;
(4) honest with you—in the nicest way;
(5) teetotal.

What we have done is to turn each of the five negative items on the list and make them positive rules of life. They certainly take on a new seriousness when we do that. You may not be quite so sure that you could lead a life acceptable to Buddhist standards, let alone accept Buddhist beliefs! We must add that Buddhist monks and nuns have five more rules on top of these—including not eating after midday!

We end with some words from Buddhist worship:

'By the Holy Path, by conquering greed, by Meditation and Wisdom, I shall teach both men and gods.'

21

The Death of Zoroaster (Parsi)

'Parsis round the world remember their Founder'
(June)

Symbol: The Parsi symbol

Music: Opening passage from Strauss's 'Also Sprach Zarathustra'.

It seems a long time now since the Apollo Moon landing and the daily news of footsteps on another world: but the theme music associated with those space age bulletins is still very much with us and can be obtained by asking for '2001, A Space Odyssey'. What is less known is that that music has its origins in Richard Strauss' tone poem: 'Also Sprach Zarathustra', and that Zarathustra was a real person, known better as Zoroaster, the founder of the Parsis.

And the trail of mystery doesn't end there either, for the Parsis are mostly to be found in India—in Bombay, where they are known as 'the Persians' or Parsis, since they fled from Persia many centuries ago, to escape the growing power of Islam. In their own country—now called Iran—they would have described .themselves as Zoroastrians, followers of Zoroaster. And they still exist today: not only in Bombay, but in the United Kingdom and other places, too. They remember Zoroaster in June and we wish them well.

Zoroaster lived about 550 BC, at a time when religious movements were lively in various parts of the world:

Isaiah was in Babylon, the Buddha and Mahavira in India, Confucius and Lao-Tse in China. Zoroaster's teaching, or at least, the part that concerns us, was simple: 'Good and evil forces are striving together for control of mankind. It is our duty to join whole-heartedly in this battle—on the side of the Good against Evil.'

The great force for Good he referred to as *Ahura Mazdah*. He likened this power to a source of light and of virtue. As such, the philosophy is not new, but in our present age, when we are tempted to refer evil, misfortune and depravity to the effects of the environment, it is well to ponder for a moment the suggestion that the forces for good and evil are real—and beyond our human strength to resist. In an age when it is fashionable to confuse 'deprived' and 'depraved', it is a sobering thought that it is a common fact of religion—not excluding Christianity—to believe in the existence of a Devil.

We don't mean by this that you should not go to bed tonight until you have searched in all the cupboards for skeletons. In any case, most of us will know that 'perfect love casts out fear'. But certainly it will repay a little consideration to bear in mind that we can fall into ways of thinking, speaking and behaving which are the fruit or the product of 'the dark side of the soul'. On the other hand, it is just as easy to blame the Devil as it is to blame our childhood, for our quick tempers, thieving hands and our come-hither looks. But Zoroaster meant what he said, and his followers were a real force for good.

Strange associations come to mind. It is almost certain that the so-called 'three Wise Men' in the Christmas story were Zoroastrians—come to satisfy themselves that the stories they had heard about a Messiah were true. It's also more than possible that the Roman army's top deity, Mithras, owes a good deal to Zoroaster. Perhaps most fascinating is the choice of the title: 'Thus

Spoke Zarathustra' by the great thinker and writer of the late nineteenth century, Friedrich Nietzsche, for his epic theory of the death of God and the rise of Superman.

Hence, probably, Richard Strauss' epic music, and the association with Apollo and the Moon Shot. Maybe Strauss' music, and Copland's 'Fanfare for the Common Man' should be issued as two 'A' sides of a single, to even the score!

Zoroaster said this:

> Who will be chosen to provide help
> through the thoughts of the good mind?
> I choose you, Lord Ahura, as my master,
> And you alone.

22

The Beginning of Ramadan (Muslim)

'Muslims prepare for the annual month of fasting and prayer' (July)

Symbol: Five-pointed Star of Islam

Music: Koran Chanting, Side 2, Track 2 from 'Religions of the Middle East', Argo ZFB 54.

Consider if you will what mighty power it is that brings about half a billion members of the world's population to their knees in prayer and fasting, for a month. What mighty force so influences men and women in every continent, speaking a hundred different languages, living in hot and cold climates, and from every walk of life, that they abstain from every kind of food and drink from sunrise to sunset for twenty-eight days?

The answer is: the word of Allah, as revealed through his prophet, and enshrined in the Koran, the sacred book of Islam. Muslims believe that the prophet Muhammad (peace be upon him), received the words of Allah from the Archangel Gabriel over a period of twenty years; and the book has become the basis not only of Islamic faith and worship, but also of Muslim daily life and education and of the unique nature of the philosophy and the legal system of Islam.

Its language is pure Arabic, or Koranic Arabic. Young Muslims learn the Koran along with their general education, and as they grow into adulthood, and take on the responsibilities of the faith, they take part in a 'growing-up' ceremony which involves chanting the Koran at the mosque. As with many other sacred books, the faithful believe that the words have divine authority only in their original Arabic language and Muslim scholars are understandably more than a little hesitant about translations. The words at the end of this talk are from an authorised translation into English by Yusuf Ali.

We haven't really answered the question: why is the Koran so effective: why is there this universal 'obedience'? The answer lies in the simplicity of the faith. Islam means surrender—in any language—and this says something very real about the nature of man which is worth your consideration.

Twentieth-century man is obsessed by his self-sufficiency, and more recently, by his increasing power over nature, not only on this planet, but beyond. Everyone knows about the most famous footsteps in history, man on the moon: 'such a small step for a man: but such a great step for mankind'. We have long since done away with 'Grace before Meals'—Perhaps we can, without offence to anyone, consider a new idea: 'Grace before Space'—or even ask whether we shall find any religion on Mars? Man, from the evidence of history, needs some kind of God: someone or something to 'surrender' to: let us dearly hope that man continues to seek this direction in his life from 'whatsoever things are good, honest and of good report'.

Here is what the Koran says about the Ramadan fast:

O ye who believe . . .
Fasting is prescribed to you:
For a fixed number of days;
Ramadan is the month
In which was set down
The Qu'ran, as a guide
to mankind . . .
So every one of you
Who is present at his home

During that month
Should spend it in fasting.
God wants you to complete
The prescribed period,
And to glorify him
In that he has guided you.

23

Dhammacakka Day (Buddhist)

'On this day, the Buddha gave his first sermon to his five followers in the Deer Park at Benares' (July)

Symbol. The Wheel of Life

Music: 'Haro No Umi', Side 1, Track 2 from 'Japanese Koto Music', Lyrichord LLST 7131.

One of the first things the Buddha did after becoming aware of the secret of good living, was to share his discovery with his closest friends.

We don't mean by this that he explained the secret! That teaching was not something he could communicate very easily to men who had not shared his unique experience: this task was to occupy him for the rest of his earthly life: a period of some forty years. In essence, the secret, as the Buddha understood it, was the transformation of the whole of your personal approach to yourself, to other people, and to life. But in that first, very important, talk to his friends in the Deer Park at Benares, on the River Ganges in North India, 500 years before the birth of Jesus, the Buddha spoke about the kind of life you should lead and the kind of person you should be.

The festival that Buddhists celebrate on Dhammacakka Day recalls the scene in the Deer Park and the words the Buddha spoke: words so simple, that we present them now, without comment. What follow are the words of the Buddha himself, ringing as true as ever, 2,500 years later (note that he mentions himself several times).

'My brothers:
Now that you have turned your backs on ordinary life,
There are two particular ways of living that you must
   avoid;
First of all, do not get into the habit of doing things
Just because they make you 'feel good',
Or because you get emotional or physical
   satisfaction. . . .
Secondly, avoid the habit of living a life that is too
   strict.
It will hurt you, and is just as unworthy of you:
This will do you no good either!
There is a way of living, my brothers,
Which avoids both of these.
It was discovered by the Buddha,
Who made a point of following it in his own life.
It is a way of living
Which makes you see the world more clearly,
Helps you understand the world better,
Gives you peace of mind,
Makes you wiser,
Helps you find 'the Truth' . . .
And takes you to freedom from earthly life. . . .
Learn to understand the Buddha's teaching.
Have a good sense of what is right in daily living.
Be careful how you speak.
Be careful how you behave.
Follow an occupation suitable for a Buddhist.
Follow the Buddha's example, as far as you can.
Learn to control your thoughts.
Try to learn the art of meditation.

The pieces of advice in the last part of the talk are called 'The Eight Noble Ways of Life' and the advice about avoiding the extremes of self-satisfaction and austerity are called 'the Middle Way'. They evoked a response in the first Buddhists and to this day their most common statement of faith is the following, the nearest we can get to a Buddhist 'Creed':

I go to the Buddha for guidance.
I need the teaching of the Buddha to help me.
I find inspiration in the good lives of the monks
Who follow the teaching of the Buddha.

24

Obon (Japanese)

'In Japan, families prepare to welcome their ancestors' (July)

Symbol: Japanese Gateway Symbol

Music: 'Peach Blossom Time', Side 2, Track 3 from 'The Chinese Violin', Candide CE 31037.

'You're a fool if you dance, and a fool if you watch.
You're a fool either way, so you may as well dance.

That's a little bit of Japanese humour for your entertainment and your further reflection. It's part of a 'Bon Song'—the words of a 'Bon Dance'. The Bon or Obon festival is all kinds of things rolled into one: a little bit of 'midsummer madness'; the beginning of autumn; welcome to the family ancestors for the annual get-together of the living and the dead; time to spring-clean so that house is fit for visitors; hope that the ancestors will bless the family and bring good luck for another year.

There is a considerable amount of Buddhism in the ideas behind the Obon Festival and much traditional Japanese culture. Specially interesting are the preparing of the road their ancestors will use as they approach the village, lighting fires by the front of the house to show them where to go, and especially by their tombs—and also the provision of lanterns in the rooms set aside for the ancestors during their stay, fresh water for them to ease their weary feet and, most important, the 'Bon shelf', with its offerings of food, drink and flowers. Guides go out to help the ancestors make the last few yards—pointing, clapping, and offering an arm or shoulder—and a few days later there are the ceremonies marking the ancestors' departure for another year. The dancing is for the delight and entertainment of the ancestors:

'You're a fool if you dance, and a fool if you watch.
You're a fool either way, so you may as well dance.'

And what is all of this to us? To be perfectly frank, by comparison with what we have just described, we positively neglect our dear departed! But then, we think of them differently. For some, death in the family is a wound that never heals: with an elaborate funeral, lengthy entries in the 'In Memoriam' columns in the Press, and perhaps a notable memorial, high, wide and inscribed at length; at home, the place always laid at table, the chair never used and the feeling of continued presence. It would, to others, be incongruous to engage in practices like those—an imposition upon a fond memory—and the anniversary of death will pass as a sad thought in the night.

So, as so often, we meet, in the Bon Dance, something probably quite unfamiliar—as strange as it would be to have a party every July, and actually expect that all the departed, both ancient and recent, will be among the company.

If you were asked by a young child: 'Where has Granny gone?', you might say: 'She has gone to be with Jesus,' or 'She has gone to sleep'—and we have that tender phrase, 'I "lost" my husband.' Everyone to their own special thoughts, especially in a sensitive and personal moment like close personal bereavement. But if you are tempted to feel that tears are natural and proper, do remember that in Japan the natural and proper things on the annual festival of the ancestors are lights, music, laughter and dancing—even party games, a tug-of-war, hurling torches, giving presents—and a special place in the festivities for the children and their particular forms of enjoyment.

As with so many religious occasions, Mother Nature is included with autumn following summer as the year begins to turn.

Here is a Japanese poem, which evokes the mysticism of life in nature:

In the land of Yamato, the mountains cluster.
But the best of all mountains is Kagu, dropped from
heaven.
Over the broad earth smoke-mist hovers.
Over the broad water seagulls hover.

25

Raksha Bandhan (Hindu)

'Brotherly love and the unity of the family in the world of Hinduism' (August)

Symbol: 'OM' symbol

Music: 'Duhn', Side 2, Track 1 from 'This is the Music of India', Philips 6460 854.

By the laws of heredity and of averages, a great many of us have brothers and sisters. If you have brothers and sisters, 'do you love them?' Do you always wish them well—in your heart? Surely you would be upset if they were hurt in any way, wouldn't you? Or again: 'do you *like* them?' Do you 'get on' with them? This is not the same thing as loving them. Can you see the difference? Can you understand that you can love someone, even though you don't always see eye to eye with them?

Well, in August at the *Raksha Bandhan* festival Hindu girls are busy tying red or gold thread round their brothers' wrists and the boys are, in turn, promising to protect them, wherever they are. So we have a custom which spotlights an aspect of human life—of family tradition, which we tend either to neglect or take for granted.

But bear in mind that in traditional Hindu life, girls are particularly at risk—they often marry, quite young, someone of their parents' choice, and sometimes find themselves widowed at an early age—sometimes with no children. It is customary for sisters to marry in order of age, and younger sisters have to wait until the older ones have married before their turn comes. The oldest generation in a family is usually the guiding authority, so the death, successively, of grandparents and parents, will sometimes leave sisters—the younger women of the house, suddenly very much alone. That's where the brothers come in—and you can see how important they are. It is so very often the brothers who take on this responsibility of love and protection.

This is summed up, as so frequently in Hinduism, by a phrase used traditionally, in the house, to describe the younger girls: 'Kanya Devi': 'girl-goddess of the House'. It's also reflected in the myths told in the family, about the privileged position of girls in the 'old days of India':

> Her father protects her in childhood,
> Her husband protects her in her youth,
> Her sons protect her in her old age

Indeed, some Hindu families practice a form of *purdah*, whereby the woman is hardly seen for the many folds of her *sari* and her head scarf of *dupatta*. This is not a selfish act of possessiveness, but more an act of protection for her in the streets of the village or, more often, the city, where those who pass by are often from many different cultures and codes of morality. This is not the time and place to introduce thoughts about the place of women in our society, but it would not come amiss to list some of the customs and courtesies which used to mark, not the weakness and inferiority of women, but rather, her natural charm and her central place in the family—no marks for success in the following list—just reflection on a passing age, not helped by the eagerness of some of our ladies to see it pass! We refer to the helps and courtesies that ladies used to receive from their brothers, fathers, sons, friends, acquaintances and complete strangers: the offering of a seat to a lady on a crowded bus; the men walking near the gutter lest mud should be spilled over the ladies by passing traffic; being served before the men at a meal; having doors opened and a way clear to pass; never being asked her age, and always being assumed to be 'only just twenty or twenty-five or, at the most, thirty (and a few months . . .)'.

The last word belongs to the Hindu young man, securely tied with red or gold ribbon, making promises to the 'Girl-goddess of the House: Deviji, Kanya Devi'.

26

Krishna's Birthday (Hindu)

'Hindus celebrate the birth and childhood of their favourite Lord' (August)

Symbol: 'OM' symbol

Music: 'Krishna, Krishna', Side 2, Track 2 from 'Ravi Shankar's Music Festival from India', Dark Horse Records AMLH 22007 (A & M Records). (Where the vocal part in 'Bhajan' starts.)

Hindus call Krishna's birthday *'Janam Ashtami'*. They keep a watch-night vigil of prayer and celebrate Krishna's birthday strictly on the stroke of midnight. They also pass the time re-enacting stories about the birth and the early years of the life of Krishna.

People have often described Krishna—but that's no wonder—he is the favourite Lord of Hindu Worship. Notice the word 'Lord': it would have been easier to say 'god', or to say 'hero', but to a Hindu, Krishna is not only a god and a hero, but also, and this is the point, he is neither a god nor a hero! It all sounds very confusing, but it's no problem to Hindus!

We mustn't allow ourselves to be worried by difficult words about religion, but they may help us to see whether there is a similar confusion about Jesus. In fact, of course, Christians, believe that Jesus is fully God and fully Man—God *and* a hero. But it's useful to consider now and then whether perhaps the disciples *gradually* discovered that the man from Nazareth was no ordinary man—but was God, no less, in human form.

It's a bit like that with Krishna—but there are still

plenty of differences. In fact, the proper title for Krishna is an 'Avatar of the god Vishnu', a manifestation of the god.

But let's continue with the birthday and its stories! When Krishna's mother had conceived him, for nine months she was surrounded by a radiance so strong that people had to shade their eyes. When Krishna was born, at midnight, the whole earth was bathed in moonlight, there was no breeze—everything was still; heavenly angels sang, and flowers fell in cascades from the sky.

Krishna's skin was dark, like a lotus leaf—and that is how he is portrayed in Hindu poster-pictures of him—you can pick him out in a crowd without any difficulty. He grew up among the cattle-grazing community of Vrindaban and Hindus positively enjoy telling the stories of his childhood. Perhaps I should hasten to add that these stories are not just curiosities, made up for the fun of it—they can be found in ancient texts, like the *Vishnu Purana*, and the *Bhagavata Purana*. Well, for a start, he overturned a wagon on one occasion—breaking all the clay pots and pans. He stole butter, pulled cows' tails and pulled up trees. Then, he played tricks on people: stealing the cowherds' pipes, driving the new calves out onto open pasture, where they could easily get lost, and distracting the milkmaids from their work by dancing with them.

As he grew older (and this is the point of the whole thing), in spite of his quite outrageous ideas about fun and games, everyone recognised the god-nature in him. But they recognised it through his irresistable humanity. Cow-girls swooned as they danced with him, seeing in him the embodiment of Divine Love.

Hindus would say 'surely God can play sometimes?' In fact, like the Greeks, the Hindus even had a special word for it: 'Lila': the Eternal Play of God with man.

In the *Gita* (a kind of Hindu 'Bible'), Krishna says

these words, which sum up what *Janam Ashtami* is all about:

> I love you well: keep me in your mind . . .
> Love me and worship me . . .
> So will you come to me . . . for you are dear to me.
> I will keep you from all that hurts: cast your care on
> me.

27

Harvest (Christian)

'Christians thank God for the Harvest, offer him harvest gifts, and share their rejoicing with the sick and needy' (September)

Symbol: The Cross

Music: 'Resurrexit' from Bach's B Minor Mass.

The traditional Harvest Festival is one of the most curious days in the Christian calendar. For most people, whether they go to church or not, it seems the most natural thing in the world to thank God for the crops and for the skill and hard work of the farmers. Sadly, the reality of the matter is that year after year the crops are a cause of grave anxiety to the farmers, and it always seems as though the weather is getting worse every year. We either have endless wet weather, or high winds or a drought. Any one of these is enough to cause a farmer's heart to miss a beat. Some of them are not quite sure, by the time September comes, whether they want to celebrate harvest at all!

Recently we have seen additions to the traditional Harvest Festival offerings which, carefully arranged for God's glory and for the joy of the occasion, include: corn, bread, fruit and vegetables; we have seen the addition of tins: tinned fruit, tinned vegetables, rice, custard and beans. We have even seen the work of men who are not farmers: wood and metal objects, clothes, plastics, farmers' tools. But everywhere, flowers. And this is right and proper, especially if the meaning of it all is to praise God for the skills of man and to offer him the 'first-fruits' of his love.

And it's right too for these things to be given away to those who sorely need them. This way, the whole community can share in the rejoicing.

But there's nothing specially Christian about Harvest Thanksgiving. In ·fact, sowing and reaping, and the weather, are probably the most common, and the most ancient, aspects of most of the world's great religious traditions. Many religions of the ancient world and many that still survive in the unspoiled parts of Africa, Asia and America are built round the annual cycle of nature: to ordinary· men and women, the passing of winter, the spring sowing and the harvest, never ceased to be a miracle, and they thanked God for it.

It was almost as though God himself 'died' and rose again with the seasons: in fact there are historical accounts of religions based on the idea of a dying and rising God. And if that reminds you of Easter, then your thoughts are exactly on the right lines. Jesus said that a seed will only grow if you bury it in the ground: and you will remember that he was a Jewish rabbi. The Jewish equivalent of Easter was partly the celebration of the beginning of the barley harvest and the Jewish equivalent of Whitsun was partly the celebration of the end of the barley harvest.

But for Christians there are two choices: you can either just thank God for another good harvest (hopefully) and for the labours of the farmers: in which case, you are joining with many millions round the world, in many religious faiths, who are doing it too. Or you can think about what Jesus said: 'A seed only grows if you bury it'. For you, this means that (to quote Jesus again) your only hope of saving your soul, is to lose it. This is very difficult to understand with your mind, but deep down inside you may find that it rings true: Jesus's life was renewed, at Easter, because he allowed that life to be buried under the crushing weight of other men's needs. He *was* the seed and the harvest is eternal life.

28

Id-ul-Fitr (Muslim)

'After a month of fasting and prayer Muslims the world over rejoice and renew their faith' (September)

Symbol: Five-pointed Star of Islam

Music: 'Call to Prayer', Side 2, Track 1 from 'Religions of the Middle East', Argo ZFB 54.

The people who are called Muslims are followers of a religion and a way of life called Islam. To a Muslim of course, there is no distinction between religion and life: the whole of life: work, worship and pleasure, is an act of *Islam*, of *submission* or *surrender*, to the will of Allah.

The claims that Muslims make about the world and about history are far-reaching but they are, in Muslim terms, reasonable and justified. The will of Allah for the world has always existed: but was not fully understood by man until six centuries after the birth of Jesus. The prophet Muhammad (peace be upon him) received the Message of Allah and this message is now enshrined in the Koran. The Koran is the source of guidance for Muslims about every aspect of life: about what to believe, how to worship in the mosque, what should be done at the various important turning points in life: birth, marriage and death, and about the giving of alms to the poor and the sick, about fasting and about making pilgrimage to Mecca. The Koran is very much in the minds of Muslims at the festival of Id-ul-Fitr.

The Festival also marks the end of thirty days of

fasting. During the Muslim month of Ramadan healthy Muslims must avoid any kind of food or drink between sunrise and sunset. If Ramadan falls in the summer months, daylight is long, and the fast is hard. If Ramadan falls in the winter, the weather is cold and again the fast is hard. But hard or not, this is the will of Allah and his followers submit, in faith. But when Ramadan is over, Muslims permit themselves a little festival: *Id-ul-Fitr*, and they enjoy themselves. They send each other '*Id*' cards—just like the greetings cards we send. For three days they engage in festivities, visit the mosque, buy new clothes and give each other presents.

There are important Muslim associations in British big cities, and a splendid new mosque in London. It is unfortunate that we have tended to refer to some immigrants by the countries we think they come from: 'Indians, West Indians, Pakistanis'. It is well to bear in mind that there are Muslims in every country, just as there are Hindus, Sikhs, Jews, Buddhists and many others. So we think now of Muslims, wherever they may be: in Pakistan, Bangladesh, the African Continent, Egypt, Java, the United States, and Great Britain; we wish them well on the occasion of their festival. Consider these words from the Koran.

Ramadan is the [month] in which was set down the Qur'an, as a guide to mankind, also clear [signs] for guidance and judgement [between right and wrong] . . . . (*A. YUSUF ALI*).

O My Lord! Let my entry be by the gate of truth and honour, and likewise my exit by the gate of truth and honour; and grant me from thy presence an authority to aid me. (*A. YUSUF ALI*).

29

Birthday of Confucius (Confucian)

'In China Confucius is remembered with respect and affection' (September)

Symbol: The Yin and Yang Symbol

Music: 'Peach Blossom', Side 2, Track 3 from 'The Chinese Violin', Candide CE 31037.

Our impressions of China are bound to be based on what we know from the news, from our popular Chinese restaurants and the amount of consumer goods that come our way from China and other parts of the Far East. This festival is about one aspect of Chinese life and Chinese history: but perhaps we ought to begin by saying that in China today people are, of course, Communist in their approach to life, although there are still some Christians there, too. But in their personal lives, many Chinese are still strongly Buddhist at heart. They also have great respect for the teaching of Lao Tse. But what is interesting for us is that many of their views about daily life are directly due to a man who was born in 551 BC—that's 2,500 years ago!

By the way, that particular period was a vintage time for religious leaders: Jeremiah was in Israel, Zoroaster in Persia, and the Buddha in Northern India: maybe there is some connection!

Confucius or K'ung was born into a poor family—the youngest of twelve children and ten of them were girls. Soon after he was born, his father died, and his mother valiantly strived to see K'ung well-educated—and succeeded! There's no doubt that young K'ung was clever and his particular interests were literature, history and social and political administration.

He gathered a circle of intellectual friends and gained for himself a considerable reputation, particularly for the extreme clarity of his thinking and the splendid simplicity of his teaching: he had a gift for expressing profound thought with an extreme economy of words. This is the aspect of K'ung's fame which has come down to us so strongly today: so much so that in some circles it is the custom to preface any outrageous remark with the words 'Confucius he say . . .'!

Well, be that as it may, K'ung did in fact, say a great deal, and became known as 'K'ung the Philosopher' or K'ung-fu-tse. Missionaries from the West who couldn't get their tongues round it, made it into a kind of reconstituted Latin: Confucius.

And now, after that substantial build-up, we must realise that Confucius was not religious: in fact, he never discussed religion. Some time after his death, as so often happens, people wanted to thank him, seek his advice and revere his memory, and, almost inevitably, he was treated as a god, and temples were built in his name. It's almost certain that if we could only hear it, there is a particularly pithy saying of K'ung's about that! So why this popularity? Why the centuries of fond memory? And why in China?

The answer is his relentless pursuit of reasonable justice and fair dealing. He secured a succession of local government posts, and in each case he sought to put right legal and social malpractice, revolutionise the legal system, help the poor, even at the expense of the rich, and maintain the supreme authority of the traditions of his ancestors. Maybe you can see, running through the list of K'ung's aspirations, some reasons why he is revered today, in a land where religion as we know it, is, to say the least, not strong, but where social justice is paramount.

It occurs to me that it's odd to separate religion and social justice like that—but there are more places in the world than we care to remember, where religion is paramount and there is little social justice. . . .

Let K'ung have the last word—after all he *did* say a great many things (called '*Analects*'); for instance:

A good way to be polite is to be natural.
If you know what is right, and do not do it, you are a coward.
A good man makes few promises, but fulfils them all.
When you leave the house, go out as if you were meeting an important guest.
Good men say little, and act without rest.

30

Rosh Hashanah (Jewish)

'Jews celebrate their New Year' (October)

Symbol: Six-pointed Star of David

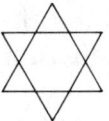

Music: 'Bereshit', Side 1, Track 5 from 'Religions of the Middle East', Argo ZFB 54.

Once again, families of Jewish people gather at home for the New Year. At Rosh Hashanah the house is spotless, and fresh: a pretty cloth covers the table, perhaps there are white flowers here and there. The lady of the house prays quietly as she lights the evening candles: perhaps it will be a good year, next year. On the table will be all the traditional festive food and especially apples dipped in honey, to suggest the promise of happy days ahead.

But in the synagogue, the blast on the ram's horn, marking the *Shofar*: 'Ram's Horn Day', reminds everyone of sterner things. God is the Creator: and as Creator he has the right to judge. When he first Created the Universe, he looked and, behold, it was very good—but what is it now? After New Year come ten days of honest self-examination. Sorrow for sins committed, and promises to do better.

Jews like to think of a particular Biblical character at festivals. Abraham comes to mind at *Rosh Hashanah*: the story of the sacrifice of Isaac is read in the synagogue: Abraham believes that he should offer Isaac to God in sacrifice. They go together to the place of the offering. 'Where is the offering?', asks the boy. 'God will provide', says his father. With the great sacrificial knife poised, Abraham spots an animal caught in a bush. He knows, deep down, that God has now provided, as he promised. Isaac, much relieved, learns, along with his father, a lesson, and the idea of 'redemption' was born. From that time it was the custom to redeem the firstborn by offering an animal in sacrifice. Since AD 70 of course, the Jews have not had a Temple and Micah's idea of 'self-sacrifice' has taken the place of the animal and mineral and cereal sacrifices listed in the Torah.

In our minds, arises the natural question: what does sacrifice 'do'? Certainly there is a strong sentiment nowadays that we should be responsible for working out our own sacrifices: meaning that we know well enough how clear our consciences are, so we must make our own peace with our God—or using a phrase from the world of commerce, guilt is 'not transferable'.

But these are rather involved thoughts—worth quiet consideration, but not easy to clarify in five minutes.

Let's return to the Jewish home, where tranquillity alternates with the sombre awareness of God. This is much clearer now. God's ways are clear: it's only men who make them confused. If little Johnny makes a splendid sand castle on the beach, then who has the right to destroy it? Answer: only little Johnny himself (or the sea!). The parable is simple: religious folk, particularly Jewish people, believe that God has created them. (The creation story as we know it, has profoundly Jewish origins.) This being so, then the Creator has the right of concern—in fact he has no choice but to be concerned about his creation: it is what his love for his creation makes *inevitable*. Year by year, he is concerned about his people. This 'concern' is difficult to explain and the traditional word 'judgement' doesn't fully express it.

But the Rosh Hashanah special services express it well:

> This is the day that the world was
>   called into existence.
> This day He causes all creatures to stand
>   in judgement.
> They name is merciful . . . you desire that man
>   return from his evil way.
> May all thy creatures form a single band
>   to do thy will with a perfect heart.

31

Yom Kippur (Jewish)

'After ten days of prayer and soul-searching Jewish people are once again "at one with God" '
(October)

Symbol: Six-pointed Star of David

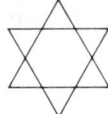

Music: 'Bereshit', Side 1, Track 5 from 'Religions of the Middle East', Argo ZFB 54.

The holiest day in the Jewish year, Yom Kippur, marks the culmination of ten days of prayer and penitence, and with its close Jews feel that they are restored, once again, to God's grace and can look forward to a fruitful and prosperous year. It may seem a strange way to begin a New Year, but in fact, the seriousness of this time for Jews, and the sincerity of their vows and their good intentions, make our more familiar 'New Year's Resolutions' sound like a children's party game!

In many ways, the Jewish New Year, which begins with Rosh Hashanah and the ten days of penitence and prayer, gets to the very core of the Jewish attitude to life and to nature. It was the 'evening and the morning' that were the first day in the biblical account of creation, not the 'morning and evening'; for Jews the evening and the night are not rewards for the hard work of the day just ended, but the proper preparation for tomorrow. Their festivals begin on the evening of the previous day, and Christians in turn have inherited the custom: Christmas Eve, New Year's Eve, All Hallows Eve (or Hallowe'en).

It's the same with seasons: their year begins with autumn and winter: hints of seedgrowth and work beneath the soil—and it is the same with the Jewish Festival Calendar. The year begins with a solemn, but honest look at your life before God. Only after ten days alone with your conscience do you feel you can set out positively on the fresh ground of a new Jewish Year.

Times have changed, of course. In the old days, when Solomon's Temple was the centre of the Jewish World, the High Priest, dressed on this occasion only in simple white garments, entered the Holy of Holies and asked forgiveness first for his own sins and then for those of the people. This was called 'Atonement', and the occasion was called 'The Day of Atonement': *Yom Kippur*. Nowadays, Jews make their own prayers and attend worship in the synagogue. Fasting marks the mood of serious concern, but we must not imagine that the Jews are sad: tears are so often marks of self-pity and they are not sad in this sense at all: simply aware of the frailty of human nature and the need for God's blessing.

In old Jerusalem at the end of Yom Kippur, the Temple gates closed: the time for penitence was over and the sounding of the ram's horn signified the return to work and the daily round of life.

Jewish people are persons of great good humour and, above all, have a realistic view of their own lives and the prospects for Jewry round the world. Yom Kippur also signifies the New Year for Jews world-wide and one never ceases to wonder at the steady continuance of Jewish life and culture. Perhaps, as with Muslims and Hindus, the secret lies in the home, where, every week at Sabbath Eve, the lady of the house presides over the family.

32

Durga Puja (Hindu)

'For many millions of Hindus, the festival of Durga means family reunions and a special kind of "Mother's Day" ' (October)

Symbol: 'OM' symbol

Music: 'Dhun', Side 2, Track 1 from 'This is the Music of India', Philips 6460 854.

Year in, year out, Hindus preserve their own colourful culture; celebrate their festivals and observe their customs. But with characteristic warm-heartedness they are always pleased to share their festivals with visitors, and *Durga Puja* is no exception.

In common with some other great religions, they find it easy to worship God under many forms and it's not surprising to find that they have a special devotion to the Great Mother Goddess: Durga. Once a year they have a festival—a *puja*—in her honour. The accent is on motherhood: families come together, and daughters in particular make a point of visiting their mothers. This underlines an important feature of Hinduism: the importance of the family and the home. The mother of the family has a special place and receives reverence and respect from her children, who speak of her as *Mattaji*: not just 'Mother', but 'honoured Mother', and sometimes as *Deviji* which means 'dear Goddess'.

The home is the place where the family pray and meditate together at the little household shrine, with perhaps a statue of Durga or of Krishna or Lakshmi, a little incense, lights, offerings of fruit and melted butter—and the chanting of ancient Sanskrit hymns which have never lost their meaning:

> Let us think, quietly and slowly, about the warm,
> Bright, light of the sun . . . .
> May the sun-god, Savitri, be our example,
> And may our minds, too, be bright.

The River Ganges, too, is a Mother, in the mind of the Hindu, representing as it does the ebb and flow of life. For Hindus the life we live is but a step—one life in a series of very many lives. The past, the present and the future mean less to them than they do to us and at Durga Puja they remember, as if it were only yesterday, the dramatic story of the *Ramayana*, which is, briefly, as follows. Vishnu, who is God in his aspect as the giver and sustainer of life, walks on earth as Rama the hero. His wife Sita is carried off by the demon Ravana and the story tells how Rama searched the length of India to find her. At last, with the help of the animals in the forest, he rescues her, and they settle, happily ever after on the great island we know as Sri Lanka. You can imagine how popular the story is with Hindu children, especially the part where a horde of monkeys make a living bridge with their own bodies, from mainland India to the island!

Hindus see life in everything around them. There is a great oneness in the universe, and that oneness is God. A Hindu finds peace when he puts his everyday life aside and finds and lives within that inner oneness with God.

> Talking about God is difficult:
> Trying to imagine him is difficult. . . .
> Just tell yourself: 'He's simply there!'
> Just saying 'He's there' is enough.
>
> *(Katha Uparishad)*

33

Divali (Hindu and Sikh)

'New Year's Day in India—a Festival of Light with lights in every home for prosperity' (October)

Symbol: The Sword symbol

Music: 'Duhn', Side 2, Track 1 from 'This is the Music of India', Philips 6460 854.

Divali is really a festival of India: it's India's New Year. Hindus and Sikhs enjoy every minute of it. In Indian craft shops you can buy attractively simple little clay saucers, complete with tiny twists of cotton wool. Hindus have lots of these around the house at Divali time, filled with oil and lit to give a soft glow in the gathering darkness of the evening.

God helps man to prosper, in the form of Lakshmi, and Lakshmi, the goddess of prosperity, will come where the lights are lit to guide her. Everyone exchanges good wishes and says: *'Namaste'* (Greetings) and 'Happy New Year'.

Some five centuries ago a Hindu called Guru Nanak, led a small group of followers which gathered strength and numbers, and we know them now as the Sikhs, who respect aspects of both Hinduism and Islam, but in particular the idea of the Truth. Life was not easy in the Indian 'middle ages', and at Divali Sikhs, again, with many flickering lamps, remember a great leader: Guru Hargobind, who was released from prison on this day.

The home of the Sikhs is the Punjab (which lies partly

in Pakistan and partly in India) and it is there that the Golden Temple of Amritsar marks the centre of the Sikh world. At Divali the Golden Temple (or *gudwara*) is festooned with lights which glitter and sway in time to their reflection in the lake around the temple.

Like the Hindus, the Sikhs are known for their good humour, their warm friendship, and their zest for their faith. When a new Sikh *gurdwara* is opened, those present often include Christians, Jews, Hindus and Muslims, as well as the whole Sikh community. The worship is composed entirely of praise and thanksgiving, with energetic and most attractive music. Apart from thanksgiving for the new temple, other prayers are offered for help and guidance in helping and protecting the young, the sick and the elderly. Above all, the central theme is Truth and that is the name they give to God.

Let us leave our Hindu and Sikh friends to enjoy Divali. The first reading that follows is from a Hindu sacred text and the second from the Sikh Holy Book, the *Guru Granth Sahib.*

Don't do your duty with your mind on the results of your actions. Never think that you yourself are the cause of the results of what you do. And don't be lazy either—shirking your duty is just as bad. Never give up doing your duty: keep your mind on God.

If I please my God, then I wish only to make my pilgrimage to the waters of his temple and be washed clean.
If I do not please my God, where can I go to find sacred water to wash away my sin? . . . All good comes from one great river of goodness. . . .

34

All Saints and All souls (Christian)

'Christians thank God for all the Saints and pray for the Souls of the Departed' (first days of November)

Symbol: The Cross

Music: 'Dies Irae' from Britten's War Requiem.

Everybody has heard of Hallowe'en, though not everyone can spell it and very few have much idea what it's about except that it's to do with ghosties and beasties: and we'll have to make it clear, unfortunately, that the 'ghostie and beastie' brigade are way off the mark! The fun and the fear that are associated with the evening of October 31st probably date way back to the celebration of the Celtic New Year, or *Samuin*. On that night, it was believed that supernatural forces were active. The best way to deal with that was to have a party, especially if there were some cattle to be slaughtered: all the best ingredients for a barbecue.

Of course, the story of Christianity in Britain is closely bound up with other things, including the left-overs of Celtic and Roman religion. We have to try to sift out the Christian bits. But perhaps we can start round about the time of the Norman Conquest—1066 and all that. Round about that time, Christians began to keep November 1st as a feast in honour of saints and heroes, and November 2nd as a day of prayer for everyone (all souls) who had died and was awaiting God's judgement.

As so often with festivals, the Bible doesn't say very much about 'All Saints' and 'All Souls', but that's because the Bible (the New Testament part, that is) was written only just after the church was born, and festivals take quite a long time to grow.

What are 'saints' and 'souls'? Saints (holy people: from the Latin word *sanctus*: meaning holy), are people who are believed to have had special blessings from God; their lives are so full of good deeds and they are such wonderful people that they go straight to God when they die and are happy there, now and for ever. And because they are to near to God, they can ask him things, ask him to bless Christians in a variety of situations: for instance. Jesus's mother, Mary, is asked, many times a day, by millions of Christians, to pray for them, now and at the moment of death. The prayer is called the *Angelus* or *Ave Maria*. Saint Christopher (the word means: 'the man who carried Christ') is believed to be particularly concerned about travellers, but I understand that he is not interested in men (or women) who drive at more than 70 mph on the M1. St Valentine has a soft spot for lovers. Hence another tradition, involving a party or a disco. And have you noticed how so many of these parties happen on the previous evening. There's something special about staying up half the night just before a day like St Valentine's Day, New Year's Day or All Saints' Day.

'Hallow' is an old English word for holy. 'All Hallows' means holy. It's the same with the Lord's Prayer: 'Hallowed be thy Name'. Hallowe'en is the Eve of All Hallows or All Saints' Day.

November 2nd is All Souls' Day. Many Christians are particularly serious on this day and go to church to hear Mass, or say prayers, for those who have died and are probably waiting for Judgement Day. Many people who die could use a few prayers! Christians pray for the 'faithful departed'—but what about the unfaithful departed? What do Christians really believe about those who die without faith? Those who die suddenly without a chance to face the future? It's a sobering thought. A 'Requiem Mass' is a service just for this purpose: and there'll be millions of Requiems on All Souls' Day this year as always.

35

Id-ul-Adha (Muslim)

'Muslims rejoice in celebration of the sacred shrine at Mecca' (November)

Symbol: Five-pointed Star of Islam

Music: Koran Chanting, Side B, Track 2 from 'Religions of the Middle East', Argo ZFB 54.

A common feature of the great religions is pilgrimage: Hindus to Benares or Vrindaban, Christians to Jerusalem, Canterbury or Lourdes, and Muslims to Mecca.

For a Muslim, pilgrimage (or *hajj*) is a sacred duty, undertaken with joy and devotion, without regard for rank or nation: an occasion when the sheer nearness of the great shrine at Mecca (the *Ka'aba*) overshadows all other thoughts. It is an experience of a lifetime and one which most Muslims can only manage once in their lives.

No wonder that, on their return, they want to celebrate, and no wonder that the Muslim world wants to celebrate with them. The celebrations often last four days: four days of festivities in the mosque, and holiday mood at home: new clothes, eating together, sharing good things with the poor and the sick, and remembering the great traditions of Islam the world over.

Muslims believe that Abraham built the great shrine, the *Ka'aba*, in Mecca, on the site of a spring (called *Zem-Zem*)—a word probably derived from the sound it made. To celebrate its completion, it is believed that Abraham made a sacrifice, and this sacrifice is specially remembered at Id-ul-Adha. Abraham was also to make a sacrifice, at God's command, of his son Ishmael, but God substituted a sheep, and Ishmael was saved.

This festival is the only occasion when Muslims are allowed to make sacrifices. The meat of the sacrifice is shared between the family, near relatives and poor folk nearby.

But it's the procession circling round the Ka'aba that is the indelible memory of Id-ul-Adha. In simple white garments, many thousands of pilgrims make their way in continuous procession, waiting their turn to kiss the precious stone which is the holiest spot in the great central square in Mecca. Rich and poor, Eastern and Western, old and young, mingle with a single thought: the nearness of Allah: the greatness of the Prophet. And this is the message for us. Our society lacks that single binding force that gives stability and direction to men's lives. Perhaps even more important, men and women lack that singleness of purpose that draws their bodies, minds and emotions together, and helps them to live balanced lives.

It would be inappropriate to suggest what that personal or social binding force should be: but what does seem true is that some kind of 'power for harmony' is indispensable for the health of humanity. We spend so much of our time working against each other and against ourselves: it's an outrageous misuse of the enormous reserves of energy that we have nowadays, when the hours of work are less and the hours of leisure often more than we know how to use.

The Prophet Muhammad (peace be upon him) is believed to have left many sayings, which are treasured by Muslims: they illustrate my point better·than we ever could: the actual words are taken from a collection made by Muhammad Amin:

He who wisheth to enter Paradise at the best door
must please his father and mother.
God is not merciful to him who is not so to mankind.

A giver of maintenance to widows and the poor like a
  bestower in the road of God, an utterer of prayers all
  the night, and a keeper of constant fast.

And finally, this is what the holy Koran says, about
the pilgrimage to Mecca (in the translation by Yusuf Ali):

Complete the Hajj in the Sacrifice of God.
But if ye are prevented: send an offering for sacrifice,
Such as ye may find. . . .
And if any of you is ill, in compensation
Either fast, or feed the poor,
Or other sacrifice.

36

Guru Nanak Day (Sikh)

'Guru Nanak was the Founder of the Sikhs—every year, Sikhs around the world celebrate his birthday' (November)

Symbol: The Sword Symbol

Music: 'Dhun', Side 2, Track 1 from 'This is the Music of India', Philips 6460 854.

Over the years, the Sikhs of the Punjab have taken their place quite firmly in our society. Of all our guests from other faiths they are perhaps the easiest to recognise: the ladies wear typical Indian dress, colourful but modest and the men wear turbans—or perhaps we should say, that any male Sikh who has undertaken to live the Faith truly and honestly, wears a turban. You may see even young teenage boys wearing the turban, but please remember that this is not to show he is a Sikh! no!—the reason is really very simple: it is to keep his hair in place!

When a young man makes his vow to be a member of the Sikh brotherhood, which they call the *Khalsa*, he takes the name *Singh* (which means lion): girls can also take the ceremony and they are called *Kaur* (princess). He undertakes to be ready at any time to defend his Faith and his fellow Sikhs. This is a reminder of the rigours of Sikh history and the devotion to courage and truth which is characteristic of Sikhs today. He carries a small symbolic sword, wears a bangle (originally to protect his wrist in battle), a pair of shorts under his other clothes, for ease of movement in an emergency and carries a comb to deal with his hair and later his beard, which he leaves uncut. The long uncut locks are gathered on his crown and bound in the turban, which can, within certain rules, be a colour of his own choice. Not all Sikhs take the vows, but of course, it's easy to recognise those who have.

The Khalsa has been in existence for 250 years or more; and Guru Nanak lived earlier still: he was born in 1469—a Hindu, living in a mixed society of Hindus and Muslims, near Lahore, in the Punjab. It's not difficult to see why he tried to forge a new basis for the good life, based on elements from both Hinduism and Islam, but especially on the idea of truth. And the attempt was a remarkable success. Not that there was no opposition. They were hard times, and eventually the tenth Sikh leader, Guru Gobind Singh, formed the Khalsa brotherhood and introduced the ceremony of initiation, *Amrit*. He also determined that the teaching of the ten Gurus, especially that of Guru Nanak, should be the sole authority for the years to come. And so the teaching: the collected sayings of the Guru, the *Granth Sahib*, the holy book, became the leader, the teacher. The *Granth Sahib* became the *Guru Granth Sahib*.

Sikhs have few rules and regulations, but they do teach a high general standard of personal life, based on Truth.

Guru Nanak is held in great affection by his followers, especially on his birthday:

> I have met Nanak, the true Guru, the true teacher.
> My union with God is complete.
> You can be saved even when you are with
> Laughing and pleasure-seeking friends,
> Even when you are wearing fine clothes,
> And enjoying good food. . . .

> It isn't words that make a Sinner or a saint;
> Actions alone are written in the book of fate.

37

Advent (Christian)

'Christians celebrate the beginning of the Church's Year' (December)

Symbol: The Cross

Music: Part of 'Comfort Ye' from Handel's Messiah.

Advent is about getting ready, expecting, looking forward, being ready, going under starter's orders, and waiting for the gun. In fact it's about everything except what it actually means: *arriving*! This is because one of the biggest problems for the Christian church is remembering everything that is important by way of celebrations and marking the events all within the space of one year. When you consider that those events, as far as Christians are concerned, took many centuries, it's not surprising that many festivals have to celebrate several different things.

So during Advent, Christians are: preparing for Christmas (perhaps you've seen Advent Calendars, or Advent Candles); thinking about John the Baptist; remembering how Jesus's coming was foretold by the scriptures; considering Jesus's promise that he would return to earth one day; and studying the effect Jesus had on the Jerusalem of his own time, especially when he rode into the city on Palm Sunday, hailed as the Messiah (Son of David, coming in the name of the Lord). Pieces from the Bible about all of these things are read in church on the four Advent Sundays and the last passage is about John the Baptist.

Religious leaders asked John the Baptist: 'Who are you?' 'Well,' he said, 'I can tell you *this*: I am not the Messiah.'

'Well then,' they said, 'Are you Elijah, or the Prophet we are expecting?' and he said, quite simply: 'No.' He told them he was 'a voice', declaring, 'make a road for God.'

During Advent, Christians, in their own way, are preparing a road for God. This is a very important thought to carry over to Christmas. Although everyone sings carols about the child in the manger, and sends pictures of a baby Jesus to each other, the real belief of Christmas is that the baby *is* God, and his birth in Bethlehem is as earth-shaking for world-history as his arrival in Jerusalem on Palm Sunday was for the devout Passover pilgrims. It is God, who is coming at Christmas and four weeks is a pitifully short time to get ready.

The prayer on Advent Sundays says 'Put away the works of darkness, and put on the armour of light,' and the quotation from St Paul reads like the Ten Commandments: so that's the side of Advent to do with high standards of personal life.

Then there are the signposts about Christmas in the Old Testament. Christians believe that there are references to Jesus in the writings of the Jewish prophets and Paul (who was a Jewish Pharisee turned Christian) thought so too. There are also the serious thoughts that are to do with Jesus's Second Coming. The earliest Christians thought this might happen within a period of months; in fact, it is said that some of them didn't bother to buy any new clothes: they thought they wouldn't need them!

But it's John the Baptist who is the clue. It's not easy to get back to the actual events: the stories about him are told by people whose own strong faith has covered the bones of fact with the flesh of belief. But there's no doubt that John baptised people—Jewish people, who normally only baptised non-Jewish converts—because he felt that God was already on the way and the people weren't ready. The extraordinary thing is that standing in queue was Jesus, and when his turn came, both John and Jesus, at the same time, were overwhelmed by the blinding revelation that God had arrived. John was overjoyed; Jesus went away on his own for six weeks to think about it.

38

Christmas (Christian)

'Christians celebrate the Birth of Jesus Christ'
(December)

Symbol: The Cross †

Music: 'Glory to God' from Handel's Messiah.

On 25th December, Christians celebrate the birthday of Jesus of Nazareth—or perhaps I should say try to celebrate the birthday of the man they believe was God. The trouble is that everyone wants to have a good time at Christmas, and most people either don't quite understand what it's all about, or perhaps even don't care very much. And if that weren't enough, Christians themselves are not sure whether they've got the facts right and the Bible story is just a little bit confusing!

To start with, scholars think that it's almost certain that Jesus was born in the spring, when shepherds would be out with their sheep to protect them during lambing time. The first Christians didn't have Christmas as we do—in December, but they did have a festival in January, about the three wise men—but that's another story! There are lots of good reasons for thinking that the wise men came to see Jesus when he was two years old, and not at Christmas.

It was the Emperor Constantine who set up a Christian festival on December 25th—to take the place of a Roman festival. He was a Christian himself and wanted the

Roman Saturnalia to die out and this proved to be a very successful way. And we might as well add that:

(1) the bible does not mention any animals in the stable;

(2) Santa Claus is taken from the stories about Saint Nicholas;

(3) the holly and the ivy, the Yule log, the mistletoe and the rest are probably ancient left-overs from the old winter festivals of nature. That doesn't mean that they are wrong, but we do need to be careful not to confuse all these things with Jesus (who was born, by the way, about 4 BC—or 4 years 'before Christ by our calendar!');

(4) and, lastly, it does remind us that many of our carols and our Christmas cards, are not exactly birthday songs and greetings for Jesus.

So what are we left with? We're left with the most important part, which becomes refreshingly clear when we take all the rest away—and makes Christmas a true Christian festival after all.

(1) Jesus was a real person.

(2) He was born at Bethlehem, near Jerusalem.

(3) His mother was Mary.

(4) The family was poor. Joseph was a carpenter, and Jesus would normally have followed his father's trade.

(5) Jesus had, from an early age, very strong interests in what we would call 'church-work', or social work, and he became a rabbi, a Jewish teacher who travelled with his students (or disciples) from place to place teaching and helping people.

(6) What is quite extraordinary is the way that in spite of his marked unwillingness to seek any kind of special reputation, people recognised in him those qualities which convinced them that he was, as Peter said, 'the Son of God'—the one whom Jews were hoping would come: the Messiah.

So in the stable, nestling in the straw, that baby *was God*. God came to earth as a man, so that men might with his help, realise that they are divine.

39

Hanukkah (Jewish)

'A Jewish Winter Festival of religious freedom: the Feast of Lights' (December)

Symbol: Six-pointed Star of David

Music: 'Bereshit', Side 1, Track 5 from 'Religions of the Middle East', Argo ZFB 54.

The story of the Jews, from Pharoah to the present day, is a story of persecution, deliverance, disaster, victory and freedom. The Jews' God, Yahweh, is a God who does things: a God of action, seen to be continually serving and saving his people. In 164 BC, after a period of particularly harsh persecution, the Temple in Jerusalem lay spoiled and ruined, with pagan worship taking place in the Holy of Holies, and all of this under the gloating eyes of an enemy king who saw himself as God on earth. The stories in the book of Daniel were written about this time. The author seems to be saying 'If you could be as courageous and daring as Daniel, we should be rid of the foul enemy and free to live and worship as we wish.'

Someone *was* daring: someone *was* courageous: his name: 'Judas Maccabaeus'. By what seemed to be a miraculous cascade of strength he routed the intruders and reinstated the Temple as Yahweh's home in Jerusalem. It was just like the Passover, like the waters of Babylon, all over again: 'God lives, O.K.?' Imagine the feeling of real satisfaction you get when you've finished all your work for the day, had a hot bath, and eventually sit down in your own tidy home: that's how it felt in 164 BC. The Jews entered the Temple again, cleansed and ready, and by common consent decided that the event called for a celebration.

The great Temple candle needed to be lit—but there was only oil enough for one night; however dawn came, and day, and night again and the oil lasted, miraculously, for eight days—the everlasting light. Judas said: 'This shall be a Feast of Lights': and so it is. In the synagogue, and again at home, one candle is lit on the first evening, a second is added on the second day, and so on, until, on the eighth day, eight lights burn brightly in every home and every synagogue.

Of course, there are gifts, and parties, especially for the young people. There is talk of the Jews' proud history of securing religious freedom and maintaining their identity as a race, a nation, a state, and the chosen People of God.

And there is a lesson here for us. Let's face it: the dice are loaded against most of us: the odds are that unless we make repeated and continuous efforts, we shall be overtaken by the modern trend to become a cypher: a faceless member of a society which is itself without a tangible identity. But we must beware of the extreme alternative: an arrogant self-opinionated individuality based only on the illusion of identity. (Long words—but we must avoid being too blunt, perhaps offensive, by using more familiar and less endearing terms!)

No—the alternative is a quiet confidence in the worth of the contribution you make in your kind of world, together with the humility to acknowledge that this contribution is not yours, but the working of a greater power, through your life, to the greater happiness of others.

40

The Islamic New Year (Muslim)

'The first day of the Islamic New Year' (December)

Symbol: Five-pointed Star of Islam

Music: Koran Chanting, Side 2, Track 2 from 'Religions of the Middle East', Argo ZFB 54.

In AD 622 Muhammad (peace be upon him), migrated from Mecca to Medina and it was at Medina that he and his companions grew in friendship and fellowship till the time came for them to return to Mecca and make it the centre of Islam. The journey to Medina is called the *Hijra*.

It may seem strange that 600 million Muslims, all around the world, should lend so much importance to an event which looks more like a retreat than a victory. Twenty per cent of the world's population is Islamic, that is one in every five people is a Muslim—that's a lot of Muslims and yet in AD 622 the *Hijra*—the journey north from Mecca to Medina (in what is now Saudi Arabia) was a journey undertaken by a determined man of vision, Muhammad (peace be upon him), and only a small group of companions—some of them doubtless with just the odd misgiving about the future. After all, their first attempt to convince the people of Mecca to abandon pagan worship and turn to Allah, had been an almighty flop. But isn't that the point? You don't really learn to ride a push-bike until you've had your first fall; you don't really swim until you've had the experience of beginning to sink. Similarly, you don't come to grips with the magnitude of a venture involving your deepest principles and convictions, until you have taken your first blow to your confidence. It happened to Moses, to the Buddha, to Jesus of Nazareth and to the Prophet of Allah. All manner of illustrations come to mind: 'clouds with silver linings', 'the darkest hour before the dawn', 'the dark night of the soul'.

The Prophet and his companions spent their time at Medina coming to terms with their Faith, and their intent to convert Mecca. It was a time of growing self-knowledge, of mutual understanding and of prayer and meditation. Above all, it was a time for building a nucleus of a community. And religion is (or should be) about community—about living and believing together. There are many clichés about 'no man being an island', but it is true to say that even in what we like to think is the age of welfare, enlightenment and vision, many groups are simply not communities at all, but just so many islands. We are, if we are honest, afraid of submission: we would make very poor Muslims—*Islam* actually means 'Surrender'. The Pillars of Islam are the proved ingredients of strong community life as follows.

(1) *Faith*: the duty to believe what other Muslims believe—that Allah is *one*, and Muhammad is his Prophet.

(2) *Prayer*: the duty to pray five times every day, at the prescribed times of the day.

(3) *Zakat*: or 'charity': giving 2½ per cent of your savings to the poor.

(4) *Hajj*: the duty of making pilgrimage to Mecca—at least once in your lifetime.

(5) *Fasting*: taking no food or drink between sunrise and sunset during the month of Ramadan.

These five duties require a substantial supply of humility: no room for arrogant individuality here! And the system works: Islam flourishes in every country in the world—working equally well in Eastern and Western cultures, on the equator or in the temperate zones, in cities and in the desert. And we are not speaking here of stunted growth of personal qualities—indeed, were it not for the artistic, literary and technical/scientific enthusiasms of the Arabs of medieval times, we would not have the universities and colleges of technology of which we are so proud today.

The Koran says:

Thy Lord is most Generous,
Who taught by the pen,
Taught man what he knew not . . .
Man is surely inordinate,
Because he looks upon himself as independent.
Surely to thy Lord all things return.

(*Y. Usuf Ali*)

41

Bodhi Day (Buddhist)

'About 2,500 years ago the Buddha became aware of the nature of suffering—on Bodhi day Buddhists recall the occasion' (December)

Symbol: The Wheel of Life

Music: 'Haru No Umi', Side 1, Track 2 from 'Japanese Koto Music', Lyrichord LLST 7131.

Every year in December Buddhists mark the world-wide celebration of Bodhi Day: the day when the Buddha found the answer to the problems of life and death and the widespread suffering which he had seen in his wanderings in India. It all happened about 2,500 years ago: the Buddha, or rather Siddartha Gautama, to give him his name (the word *Buddha* is a title meaning 'enlightened one' or 'the one who knows'), was born into a rich princely Hindu family in Northern India in 563 BC. He turned his back on the luxury of his home, and as a young man set out to seek the meaning of the poverty, suffering, old age and death which were so painfully obvious in the society outside the grounds of the palace.

The journey was not easy: his first thought was to undertake the life and habits of a wandering holy man: perhaps a life of fasting and self-deprivation would bring him an answer and go some way to relieving other men's pain. But no answer came and his own suffering seemed only to add to the suffering of the rest. Under the shade of the great bodhi tree in Benares he finally settled his weary body, and determined to stay there until he had achieved the solution he sought: no matter how great the effort involved.

Distinguish, if you will, between two kinds of knowledge, as Buddhists understand them. We learn: we become knowledgeable, well-informed, by reading, listening, observing, being taught. Some of us find this easier to do than others: we are all different. A Buddhist would say that when we describe ourselves like this we are talking about our ego, our individuality: lively, assertive, self-protective. When a Buddhist settles down to meditate, his or her first task is to come to terms with the ego: go beneath it to the other kind of knowledge: for it is in the depths of the soul, beyond the ego: where individuality and personality have no meaning, that a certain 'wisdom' or 'intuition' resides, awaiting the moment of waking or enlightenment. The nearest we get to this in our lives is when, in a moment of self-forgetfulness, relaxation or sleep, we 'become aware' that the answer to some problem before us is something we suddenly realise we knew all the time, deep down. But these are isolated flashes of so-called 'inspiration': to have this facility ready to hand is a task not to be undertaken lightly: indeed, it is only for those who are prepared to follow the precepts of Buddhism.

The best summary of this idea is the words of a Buddhist singer:

May I turn from the world: may my meditation progress:
May I loosen my hold on the essentials of life:
May the flowers of divine visions awaken.

42

Saint's Day (Christian)

'Christians honour Holy Men and Holy Women'
(Dates throughout the Year)

Symbol: The Cross

Music: Tallis: Spem in Alium.

Ask anyone to name a few saints. The answers will probably be like this: 'Matthew, Mark, Luke and John . . . St George, St Andrew, St David . . . and St. Patrick . . . Peter, Paul . . . the twelve disciples . . . Mary . . . Christopher, Valentine. . . .' Continue the quiz: 'You've only mentioned one woman. . . .' The answer might be 'er: Mary Magdalene, St Catherine. . . .' Finish off with: 'Were there any saints before Jesus?' If the answer is 'No' it is wrong—what about St John the Baptist? And finally, 'Are there any saints alive now?' . . . 'Er: the Pope?'

Look in books about the saints (the proper word for writing about saints is 'hagiography') and you'll find hundreds of saints, men and women who are honoured in the Church's calendar, and there are very many more who are honoured by the people who remember them in the place where they lived and died.

Try going through the rhyme 'Oranges and Lemons'—there are some odd names there. Try looking up old churches: more odd names.

What is a saint? The word means 'holy', 'special', set

apart or chosen. So who is to say that someone is a saint? The formal, official way, the way it's done in the Roman Catholic Church, is for the Pope, after due discussion, to declare that someone has been 'canonised'. That means that they are believed to have gone straight to God when they died, because their lives were so obviously good, and perhaps because they died very bravely for their beliefs—we call such people 'martyrs'.

Many Christians believe that the saints not only pray to God for them, but sometimes help them directly. Perhaps the best known example of that is the enormous number of people, especially sick people, who go every year to Lourdes, the shrine of the Blessed Virgin Mary, made famous by the story of St Bernadette. There are many other stories of miracles—marvellous happenings—connected with shrines all over the world. We should be very careful not to dismiss these stories too lightly.

The God that Christians believe in has undoubtedly led many men and women to live such marvellous lives that the word 'saint' is the only word that fits them. But there are 'small miracles' in everyone's lives, and a Christian will say 'That was God, stepping into my life'.

We should learn from devout Christian people. It's very easy to make jokes about people who are religious, and mostly they don't mind, but deep down they have a link with God that other people just don't have, because they have no God, or they are too far away from him.

What are saints for? Those who believe in them never even think of asking the question!

The Festivals listed by Faiths according to the School Year

Christian
Harvest (September) (27)
All Saints and All Souls
 (November) (34)
Advent (December) (37)
Christmas (December) (38)
The Beginning of Lent
 (February) (3)
Mothering Sunday (March) (6)
Easter (April) (9)
Whitsun (May) (16)
Trinity Sunday (June) (17)
A Saint's Day (Dates throughout
 the year) (42)

Jewish
Rosh Hashanah (October) (30)
Yom Kippur (October) (31)
Hanukkah (December) (39)
Purim (March) (7)
Pesach (April) (10)
Shavuot (June) (18)

Hindu
Durga Puja (October) (32)
Divali (October) (33)
Birthday of Ramakrishna
 (February) (5)
Holi (March) (8)
Rath Yatra (June) (19)
Raksha Bandhan (August) (25)
Krishna's Birthday (August)
 (26)

Muslim
Id-ul-Fitr (September) (28)
Id-ul-Adha (November) (35)
The Islamic New Year
 (December) (40)

Birthday of the Prophet
 (February) (4)
The Beginning of Ramadan
 (July) (22)

Buddhist
Bodhi Day (December) (41)
Birthday of Shakyamuni (April)
 (11)
Wesak (May) (13)
Dhamma Vijaya (June) (20)
Dhammacakka Day (July) (23)

Sikh (*see also* Divali (33))
Guru Nanak Day (November)
 (36)
Birthday of Guru Gobind Singh
 (January) (1)
Baisakhi (April) (12)
The Martyrdom of Guru Arjan
 Dev (May) (14)

Bahai
The Ascension of Bahá'u'lláh
 (May) (15)

Parsi
The Death of Zoroaster (June)
 (21)

A Confucian Festival
Birthday of Confucius
 (September) (29)

A Festival from China
Chinese New Year (January)
 (2)

A Festival from Japan
Obon (July) (24)